The Philosophy of Music

Halbert Hains Britan

BIBLIOLIFE

THE PHILOSOPHY
OF MUSIC

*A Comparative Investigation into the Principles
of Musical Æsthetics*

BY

HALBERT HAINS BRITAN, Ph.D.

Professor of Philosophy in Bates College

LONGMANS, GREEN, AND CO.

FOURTH AVENUE & 30TH STREET, NEW YORK
LONDON, BOMBAY AND CALCUTTA
1911

To
E. F. B.,
who has helped me to see the Beauty of
Goodness and the Goodness of
Beauty, I inscribe this book.

PREFACE

In offering this book to the public, the author feels constrained to ask for it the kindly consideration usually granted to pioneer work. For while the bibliography of music is voluminous, attempts at a scientific, psychological analysis of music, and at a systematic discussion of the principles of musical æsthetics are surprisingly few. Of all the books examined, Gurney's *Power of Sound* was by far the most valuable, though its wealth of keen observations and valuable conclusions is all but buried under a great mass of needless verbiage and other forbidding infelicities of style. Under the circumstances it seemed best to the author therefore to start boldly out trusting to his psychological knowledge for chart and compass, and to his philosophical training to lead him through the subtleties and half-mystical generalities which for so long have beclouded this particular field of art.

The thanks of the author are due, and are here gratefully given to those whose sympathy has given him encouragement, and whose suggestions and criticisms have proven most valuable. Among those who have thus contributed to whatever value the book may have, mention must be made especially of Professor H. C. Macdougall, and of Professor Horatio Parker, who have kindly read portions of the manuscript and offered many helpful suggestions.

H. H. BRITAN.

Lewiston, Maine, July 14, 1910.

REFERENCES

AMBROS, *The Boundaries of Music and Poetry.*

BARTHOLOMEW, *Relation of Psychology to Music.*

BELLAIGUE, *Musical Studies and Silhouettes.*

BOLTON, *Rhythm,* "American Journal of Psychology," Vol. VI, No. 2.

BUTCHER, *Aristotle's Theory of Poetry and Fine Art.*

DAURIAC, *Essai sur L'Esprit Musical.*

EDWARDS, *God and Music.*

GOODELL, *Chapters on Greek Metric.*

GURNEY, *Power of Sound.*

HADOW, *Studies in Modern Music.*

HAND, *Æsthetics of Musical Art.*

HANSLICK, *Vom Musikalisch-Schonen*

LEE, *The Riddle of Music,* "Quarterly Review," Jan., 1906.

LUSSY, *Musical Expression.*

MONRO, *The Modes of Ancient Greek Music.*

PARRY, *Evolution of the Art of Music.*

PUFFER, *The Psychology of Beauty.*

CONTENTS

PART I

INTRODUCTION

CHAPTER I

THE PROBLEM STATED

CHAPTER II

MUSICAL FORM

PART II

PSYCHOLOGICAL ANALYSIS OF THE ELEMENTS OF MUSIC

CHAPTER III

RHYTHM

CHAPTER IV

RHYTHM (continued)

CHAPTER V

MELODY

CHAPTER IX

THE CONTENT OF MUSIC

CHAPTER X

MUSICAL CRITICISM

CHAPTER XI

THE EDUCATIONAL VALUE OF MUSIC

PART I

INTRODUCTION

CHAPTER I

THE PROBLEM STATED

1. In comparing music with the other arts three general traits are readily noted, traits which serve to attract the attention of the mind philosophically disposed, and to provoke an inquiry as to their nature, causes and significance. In the first place, music as a form of art is remarkable for its wide appeal to mankind. Now and then in the past some art has so enlisted the sympathies and energies of a people that it is not inappropriate to speak of the interest evoked as national. Such, for example, was the interest in sculpture in Greece during the Periclean age, or in painting in Italy during the hundred years ending with the middle of the sixteenth century, or in architecture under the enthusiasm of Gothic ideals.

And yet, even in the halcyon days of these arts, there was never, I venture to say, such a wide-spread interest and enthusiasm as the people of the Western world are to-day according to music in its various forms. This is due not to a wave of popular fancy, a mere society or social fad, but it will find its explanation only in a theory that shows music to be eminently adapted to be as it is to-day, the art of the age and the art of the people. Even a casual survey of the place music holds in the social life of our nation will be sufficient to convince one of its vitality and of its popularity. In our larger cities are orchestras and choral societies and opera, which, to exist under present conditions, must be generously supported; mention may be made also of countless lesser organizations and soloists, these, too, dependent for their support upon popular favor. Besides this list of professional musicians, attention should be called to the universal use of music in religious worship, in social gatherings of various kinds, in the theatre, in the army, in our schools, and in our homes, where in a large majority of cases music of some form is now cultivated. Such a survey forces the conclusion upon us that music is preeminently the art of the people and the art of the age.

Its universal character finds further confirmation in the fact, now being established through ethnic and anthropological investigations, that among all tribes and nations, in every stage of racial progress, with men of every color, temper and natural disposition, music of some form is found without exception. From the lowest stages of barbarism to the highest stratum of modern culture music has been found to play an important part in the mystical, religious, social or æsthetic life of every people. It is true that in crudity and demonstrativeness the music is closely commensurate with the development of the people in question, but this only goes to prove that the roots of music lie deep in human nature, and that music, like all other forms of mental activity, is subject to the law of development.

But even more startling and more suggestive than this universality of musical appreciation is the versatility of the art we are considering. Its remarkable adaptability to man's many and varied emotional experiences not only serves to differentiate it from the other arts, but points to some much-needed investigation of its true psychological character. Henry Van Dyke, in his recent volume of poems, in the "Ode to Music" thus poetically recognizes the wide emotional range of music:

> "Where wilt thou lead me first?
> In what still region
> Of thy domain
> Whose provinces are legion
> Wilt thou restore me to myself
> And quench my heart's long thirst?"

Then follow a Play Song in childlike simplicity; a Sleep Song of rare beauty, though studied the critics say; a Hunting Song breathing of the freshness of the morning; a Dance Song of lightness and rhythm well molded; and the Symphony expressive of the deeper æsthetical truths of the art. However, even in this varied enumeration he by no means exhausted the series, or bounded the province of this art. The inspiriting effect of martial music is too well known to need more than casual mention; its power to relieve even the most materialistic fatigue and to strengthen a lagging will is a fact which armies have long known and utilized. Of similar nature is the use of music to arouse enthusiasm upon the football field and in the old-fashioned political meeting.

Antipodal to these uses in character but no less powerful in its effect, is the place music holds in modern enlightened religious worship. Here it allies itself not with the boisterous spirit of college rivalry nor with the pugnacious instinct in man, but with the calm, emotional phenomena of religious meditation and worship. The effect desired and produced in the two cases is in striking contrast; in the former case music excites, animates the mind, and energizes the will; in the latter, it calms the soul, and brings repose and rest, turning our thoughts by the forceful beauty of its deep harmonies and sober rhythm to a more serious contemplation of the experiences of life. In social meetings, to promote good cheer and unity of feeling, music is a means never failing, never trite. In the dance, music brings gayety and exhilaration; but the dirge, or the funeral march can turn our thoughts at once from sunlight to deepest shadow. But in the strength of all these dramatic effects which music has such power to produce, it must not be forgotten that as an art music has power to rise to the sublimest heights of æsthetic form and so charms the mind by the pure beauty of its artistic qualities. This versatility, this adaptability to man's various emotional experiences without artificiality or loss of power, is another of the potent qualities of music awaiting explanation.

Again, music is remarkable not only for its universality and its versatility, but also for its *power*. No other art, with the possible exception of certain forms of literature, can make the emotions so poignantly real, or can so effectively oppose the dominance of some mood which may for the time have cast its spell over the mind. Upon this attribute of music the world has remarked and perchance reflected since the days when David took his harp to solace the heart of Saul, and the Greeks repeated and believed the myth of Orpheus and how by the magical sweetness of his music he charmed the hearts of man and beast. The fact which the ancient Hebrews thus noticed and the Greeks in their fanciful way represented in their myth, has not paled beneath the clearer light of modern scientific examination, but remains unchallenged though still largely unexplained.

Such are some of the more obvious facts which meet us when we pause for a moment to consider music as a form of art. That they are so patent does not lessen their significance, nor make a critical examination of their nature and force any the less imperative. Rather, the fact that they are so evident as to be almost commonplace serves to increase the obligation philosophy is under to investigate their nature and to find the secret of their psychological value. Philosophy like philanthropy begins best by beginning at home. This much may be given as a tentative conclusion An art that begins far back in the obscurity of the earliest forms of racial progress, and is present as a factor of increasing importance through the long ages of development to the best outcome of ethnic progress; an art that finds an immediate and a forceful response from men in every land and in every stage of mental growth and education; an art so versatile that it can arouse and stimulate almost every emotion of the human heart, and with such dramatic power; an art that in its highest artistic form is worthy to be classed with the best expression of man's æsthetic consciousness such an art is certainly not ephemeral or insignificant, but must send its roots deep into the heart of man's mental constitution and stand intimately related to the basic forms of consciousness itself.

2. As might be inferred from the last remark, musical æsthetics is a subject upon which there is a wide divergence of opinion and a very general lack of exact and lucid thought. There are several reasons why this is true. In the first place, music is by nature both intangible and evanescent, and for this reason hard to apprehend clearly without some natural aptitude or careful training. With a few paintings before him even a novice might soon learn to recognize the outward marks of a Turner or a Corot or a Monet, while only a long training would enable him to decide with equal facility whether a composition were by Schubert or Mendelssohn or Beethoven.

Then again, the symbolism in which music is expressed is incapable of being translated into our conceptual terminology. Music is the only art of which this is literally true. Word pictures will go far toward giving a fairly accurate description of the conception of any other form of art, but a melody or a musical thought is essentially untranslatable and indescribable.

Besides, music through the emotional suggestiveness of its dramatic factors lends itself readily to mystical interpretation and obscure generalities. The following quotation will illustrate what I mean "I for one know well, that, so long as my life-happenings can be conveyed fitly through words, I will not use them as a musical theme. The longing to express myself musically comes over me only in the realm of obscure feelings, at the threshold of the World Beyond, the world in which the categories of Time and Space rule no more." One cannot read very far in musical literature without meeting many times with just such expressions. They may be true in a general sense, but they depart woefully from the exactitude which a world influenced more by scientific than by poetic ideals naturally craves. We labor, therefore, against difficulties inherent in the problem, and hence inevitable.

Another reason why the philosophy of music is to-day still immature, unsettled almost as to its first principles, is found in the fact that music in its present harmonic form is still in its early maturity. Attention has been engrossed heretofore with the cultivation of music for its own sake, rather than with an attempt to understand its principles in their philosophical relations. There has been a philosophy of poetry, for example, since the time of Aristotle, but it is only in recent years that systematic attempts have been made at a philosophy of music. And, indeed, it could not have been otherwise: philosophy does not precede, but follows the actual processes of development. The data must first be supplied, and then reflected upon and unified into a coherent, logical system. Consequently philosophy has well restrained the feverish impulse to appropriate the field of music to her domain until the art itself should be mature.

But to such maturity music has now attained, and the time is at hand when music should be considered in its wider relationships. It is doubtless true that there will continue to be new movements, new schools, new ideas (for art does not seek to perfect the old, but to discover the new), but no one acquainted with the music of the last century would

dare to say that music has not attained to a vigorous and energetic maturity. If past attempts at a
philosophy of music, due to a lack of proper data,
have been sporadic and incomplete, there is no
longer a like reason why similar attempts are
doomed to failure. The present status of musical
theory and of psychological analysis is such that
the material is at hand for such a systematic study,
if we care to avail ourselves of it. What is needed
now is not greater facility in musical analysis, and
a more complete understanding of the architectonic
of musical compositions, but a more reflective study
of such data as we already possess and a synthesis
of such material with the fundamental principles of
mental activity. It will help, perhaps, to define our
problem and to show more clearly the direction in
which our goal lies if we contrast for a moment the
study of music from the standpoint of the musician
and from the point of view of a student of philosophy.

3. The musician studies music for its own sake.
If music is worthy of the place it claims for itself
in the category of the fine arts, it must have a content worthy to be compared with the best ideas and
ideals of these arts, with the content of our best
painting or of our best literature for example. It
must be an expression of some truth of Life itself,
a truth capable of being crystallized under the form
of sense beauty, and of producing an æsthetic reaction in consciousness. Music, we believe, has such a
content; to find such truth and to express it, or to
interpret it for others is the true function of the
musician. Music is no blot nor blank, it means
intensely and it means good; to find its meaning
is, for the musician, if not meat and drink, at least

his proper task. The musician, therefore, making music the constant object of his study, gets deepest into its meaning, understands best its message, and appreciates best the character of its truth. At least these are the possibilities that lie open before him.

All this, however, is not so easy as the statement might imply. While such power of direct vision may now and then be granted to some musical genius that the nature and reality of the goal be not lost to man, the usual road is one of arduous windings and many a day of rough and barren climbing. That is to say, the usual method by which musicians come to an appreciative understanding of musical composition is through the study of the technique of musical form and musical principles.

As a musician, therefore, the student of music is interested in understanding the structural elements of music in general and of different compositions in particular. He must be able to analyze a musical composition and to see how from certain elements the composer has builded the logical structure of a work of art. To do this he must have a critical knowledge of the various elements and forms of music, the uses of rhythm, the relation of keys, and of the major and the minor modes, the theory of harmony, and the principles of musical expression; he must be able to pick out the subjects of the various movements, and to recognize them in their various forms in the exposition, development and recapitulation; he must have an ear trained to appreciate delicacy of modulation and of harmony, and to recognize the more logical unity and balance of rhythmic structure. Besides all this he must-

have musical feeling, the ability to appreciate and
to express shades of feeling which are beyond the
possibility of graphical representation. As a musician merely the problem of the content of his art,
except as this term is used to denote bare sequence
of tones in succession, is extraneous to his purpose.
His end is attained when he so thoroughly understands the musical structure of the composition
that he can intelligently criticise its interpretation
and feel the emotion that inspired, or accompanied,
its creation.   True, as a man of culture or even as a
well-informed student of his art, the musician must
know something of the history of music, and of its
general significance, and yet strictly from the musician's point of view this is not essential, except so far
as such knowledge helps him to understand and
interpret the compositions in the way we have outlined above.   Let not our statement be misunderstood; we are not advocating in any sense a restric-
tion of the field of study of the musician, but merely
trying to set the limits where pure musical purposes
end and other interests begin.

The study of music from the point of view of the
student of philosophy is essentially different from
that which we have just sketched. The interests of
the musician are centripetal, while the interests of
the philosopher are centrifugal. The interest of the
former, as we have shown, centres in the art itself,
while the interest of the latter is directed outward,
seeking for points of relation between music and the
other arts and other forms of human experience.

The philosopher must recognize the right of the
musician to priority in his own field. In matters of
musical theory he can only defer to the judgment

of the musician and confess that much of the information he uses is second-hand. And yet this is no more the case with music than it is in any other branch of æsthetics or of philosophy in general.

The true function of philosophy lies beyond the immediate facts or principles which science gives. The data of philosophy are all borrowed, so no more in this instance than elsewhere. The philosopher in any branch of æsthetics is but a traveller passing through the land, not like the spies of Joshua, that he may spy it out, and return and possess it, but that he may make of it a comprehensive survey in order that his map of the whole realm of art may be complete. He will do well, therefore, to learn from musicians, the rightful owners of the soil, those facts which a life-long experience may have given them. Since he is but a surveyor, as it were, seeking for the defiles, the passes, the natural avenues of approach which connect this enchanted land of music with the outlying provinces of the other arts and of other fields of human experience, he must choose as his guide, if he show the wisdom his name implies, one whose experience has made him familiar with all the winding streams and hidden passes and fertile plains of his home land. True it may be that he has never lifted his eyes to the hills to find the sources of those enchanted streams which make his country so fair, nor followed them down to where at last they flow out into the boundless ocean of Truth; but this does not lessen his efficiency as a guide in the land in which he lives and which he knows better than any transient incomer from other scenes.

There is, therefore, no cause for enmity or jealousy between the musician and the philosopher, but every cause for hearty coöperation and mutual assistance. The philosopher must gain from the musician those data which alone make his work possible. Had he first to master completely the technical study of music, his prime purpose would be lost in the multitude of preliminary details. On the other hand, the musician, if he is to be successful in his chosen work, must confine himself to his specific tasks and not be drawn away by the allurements of philosophical theories. But when the philosopher has completed his work and has formulated his argument in a systematic way, the results of his labor should be of the greatest interest and help to the musician in enlarging the scope of his vision and in giving him clearer ideas as to the relation of music to other forms of human experience.

4. What, then, to discard our figure of speech, are some of the more specific problems which a philosophy of music must undertake to solve? Clearly, one of the chief inquiries to be raised, chief both in its inherent importance and because so much depends upon it, is to determine as clearly and as accurately as possible the nature of the psychological processes involved in the musical experience. The psychological method of investigating all phenomena connected with human thought and action has so abundantly justified itself that it here needs no defense. It is not without good and sufficient reasons that this method has become almost synonymous with scientific accuracy, and with axiomatic grounds of certainty. In the case of music the demand for the most thorough-going, critical psychological analysis is peculiarly impera-

tive, (1) because so little systematic work of this
kind has as yet been undertaken, and (2) because
the mental reactions constituting the musical experience are in many respects so intangible and subtle
that they lead readily to exaggeration and vague
generalities which in the light of a scientific psychology are either meaningless altogether or mere
platitudes. To understand in the simplest possible
terms the character of the mental reactions which
music engenders is therefore one of the most imperative problems of musical æsthetics. This can
be attained only by a critical analysis of music into
its elements and an examination of the effect of
these elements taken separately upon the mind.
In this way alone can we hope to come to a clear
and full understanding of the real nature of music
subjectively considered.

Another reason why the psychological examination of music is so important is the fact that upon
the data thus determined rests the possibility of
relating music to other manifestations of human
thought and action. In order that philosophy may
relate one subject to another, one art to another,
or to some subject apparently independent of the
one in question, it is necessary that some bond
of connection be discovered. Now psychological
analysis is the alembic modern philosophy is using
to-day and in it hopes to be able to resolve the most
refractory forms of consciousness, the most subtle
and abstract ideas and ideals. Whether or not these
hopes will ever be adequately fulfilled, it is unquestionably true that this is the best method yet discovered of attacking these more subtle problems
with which philosophy is compelled to deal. Thus

it is imperative that attention be directed first to
the psychological analysis of music not only for the
interest inherent in this problem, but also because
this is the necessary prolegomenon for the solution
of the further inquiries philosophy is ready to propound. For example, there is urgent need to-day
for the formulation of the principles upon which
musical criticism rests and by virtue of which it
has authority. As critics themselves are ready to
admit, musical criticism is not yet fully conscious
of the principles which underlie the musical art, and
as a consequence there is a notorious lack of unity
and authority in the multitudinous judgments passed
upon music. So much so that one of the papers in
our metropolis amused itself not long since by com-
piling a long list of contradictory quotations taken
from the musical criticism of its leading newspapers.
Nothing can remedy this weakness so long as there
is lack of unanimity of opinion as to the true character, purpose, and principles of music. Such an
analysis as we propose ought certainly to do something toward laying the principles for authoritative
criticism.

Passing outside of the realm of music itself to consider its relation to some other fields of human
thought, one of the first problems to propose itself is
naturally the relation of music to the other arts. As
an art with a definite character and individuality of
its own, music must have certain *differentia* by which
it is distinguished from the other arts; but, on the
other hand, it is no less evident that it must have in
common with the other arts certain essential attributes, by virtue of which it is placed in the category
of art. The *differentia*, the points of difference, are in

common thought more emphasized than the points of agreement. These are the technical attributes, the proper subject of study for the musician, and for professional schools. But for a philosophy of music it is upon the common point of agreement that attention must be centred; these latter, not the former, are the basis for a real, comprehensive understanding of music as a form of art. To point out, therefore, these common attributes and to estimate their value will prove to be not only an interesting task intellectually, but it is indispensable for a philosophical appreciation of the true character, import, and purpose of music. However, a philosophy of music will lead us farther afield than into these outlying provinces of the other arts.

Music is not morality; but from the days of Plato and Aristotle music and morality have been intimately associated both in popular and in philosophic thought. The philosopher, actuated by a dominant desire for unity, is prone to believe that the æsthetical and the ethical ideals are not only compatible, but essential each to the other. The man more pragmatically minded finds numerous inconsistencies between certain apparent results of music and the ordinary conceptions of moral practices. But the problem—surely the problem remains for him who would attack it.

Again, art is not religion, but the fact that no one of the arts in any land has risen to world renown apart from the guiding influence and inspiration of religious ideals certainly suggests that this is not merely coincidence several times repeated. And while it may be true that the great musical period of the last century received less inspiration from religious conceptions than have some of the other arts, the intimate relation always existing between music and religious worship forbids that the question of the relation between music and religion be not raised, though it receive but scanty treatment in the following chapters. If philosophy during the scholastic period was the "handmaid of religion," music must now and always be assigned a more sisterly relation to religion than philosophy ever was justified in claiming. Take away from religious worship music in all its forms and an irreparable, incalculable injury has been done.

Again, there has been during the last decade or two a strong tendency to give music a larger and larger place in our educational practices, and it is doubtful if the tide is yet at its flood. Can it justify itself there, when our courses of study are growing so fast and are even now so overcrowded that school work seems verging on dilettanteism? And if so, how? This it may be urged is more a practical than a philosophical problem, and yet it should be remembered that its solution demands just that thoroughgoing psychological analysis at which this discussion aims. It might also be urged that to-day even practical educational questions are becoming more and more problems demanding the broadest philosophical treatment The question, therefore, is pertinent as well as practical, philosophical as well as pedagogical, and may well claim our interest and attention.

Among the problems of a philosophy of music one other must engage our attention. A philosophical discussion of any subject, whether it be science or art, soon leads to a consideration of its content as the most comprehensive, the most searching inquiry

connected with the investigation. To any one acquainted with philosophical procedure, the reason
for this is obvious; the central problem of philosophy
is Ontology, or the theory of the ultimate constitution
of reality. This is essentially the problem of the
content of Nature. Now philosophy, whichever way
it turns or whatever the subject with which it is engaged, has always this question to propound, What
is the essential, irreducible content when analysis
has reduced the subject to its lowest terms?

Upon the problem of the content of music musical theorists have long been divided into two opposing schools, the "Formalists" and the "Expressionists." The Formalists, of whom Eduard Hanslick of
Vienna is perhaps the best spokesman, maintain that
the beauty of music is in the mere formal play of
musical tones in rhythmic and melodic or harmonic
progression. The favorite figure of speech of this
school is that music is an "arabesque of sound;" that
is, sound patterns intricately but logically interwoven
and interrelated. According to the contention of
those who subscribe to this theory, music is simply
what is heard or, more accurately, what the ear receives; and the whole content of music is the technical data which the musician discovers in his analysis
of various compositions. As Hanslick says: "Die
Darstellung eines bestimmten Gefuhls oder Affektes
liegt gar nicht in dem eigenen Vermögen der Ton-
kunst." . . . "Die Ideen, welche der Komponist
darstellt, sind vor allem und zuerst rein musikalische.
Seiner Phantasie erscheint eine bestimmte schöne
Melodie. Sie soll nichts anderes sein als sie selbst." [1]

The Expressionists, on the other hand, contend

[1] *Vom Musikalisch-Schönen*, pp. 26 and 30.

that music is something more—far more than an
arabesque of sound, artistic and sensuously pleasing
though it be. To regard music in this empirical fashion is to defame it and rob it of all its significance and
glory. This school, therefore, regards music as primarily a symbolic expression of inner states of feeling,
the richest and deepest the mind can know. Its
power, its significance, its glory are due to the directness and accuracy with which it can express the
yearning and longing and exultation of consciousness in its various moods.

The classical proof of this is found in such compositions as Beethoven's Pastoral Symphony, with
its "Scene at the Brook," the "Peasants' Merry-
making," the "Storm," the "Shepherd's Song," etc.
Or reference might be made to the "Program
Music" of some of our best composers who now
and then essay to picture for us some definite scene
or mood through the medium of musical symbolism. Wagner's innovation also, in which he
attempted with world-renowned success to make
sound and scene and sense harmonious, might be ad-
duced as evidence for this theory of music. Then
there is music like that of Chopin and the Romanticists in general, the effect of which is so palpably
emotional that it seems artificial to interpret it in
any other way. In the face of such examples the
formalistic hypothesis seems barren if not positively
false. The favorite figure of speech of those of this
persuasion is that music is the "language of the emotions." Thus supported by much cogent argument
on either side, the breach has widened until the extreme views just outlined have been vigorously sustained. And even though it be asserted that this is

no longer the vital problem in musical æsthetics, which is probably the truth, there is a problem here which, though it needs a new alignment, is still of great moment in a philosophy of music.

Before we take up the psychological analysis of music, it seems expedient to borrow from the musicians such data concerning the technique of music as will assist us most in getting a clearer conception of the psychological character of this art, and help us to solve the various philosophical problems we have just proposed. Such is the purpose of the following chapter.

CHAPTER II

MUSICAL FORM

1. Every work of art, if its true character and
its full significance are to be apprehended adequately,
must be considered from two distinct points of view,
viz., the objective and the subjective. 'From the
objective point of view a work of art is a concrete,
sensuous form and must as such exemplify certain
sensuous but æsthetic attributes.' When regarded
in this way, attention is centred most naturally upon
its objective or structural, and upon its obvious,
sensuous attributes. Beauty, to one who looks out .
from such a standpoint, will seem to lie entirely in
these sense qualities and to be explained by attributes of sense entirely. Thus a painting, for example, shows colors harmoniously blended, light and
shadow, forms suggested or accurately drawn, composition, balance, etc , all objective attributes and,
to a certain extent, to be appreciated and judged
upon their sensational value.

But a work of art is also, at the same time, a symbolic form to be interpreted and enriched from the
inner life and experience of the beholder. From this
point of view the objective form is but a skeleton, a
symbol, a sign to be interpreted not in terms of objective reality, but in terms of the inner life of consciousness. "From the heart it sprang and to the
heart it must appeal," said one of the masters of one of

his compositions. Under this mode of envisagement the subjective experience, not the objective form, assumes the place of prime importance. Neither of these two ways of regarding art is superfluous, nor is the whole truth to be gained from either standpoint alone, try as we may. Much confusion in æsthetics has resulted from a failure to observe this truth. In justice to the subject, and certainly in the interests of the fullest conception of art and the truth it portrays, the fact must be recognized that both points of view are valid and complementary. The Hegelian method has not been rendered obsolete by the modern experimental method of investigating the problems of art. This chapter, it is evident, will have to do primarily with the objective characteristics of music.

Regarded objectively, each art has its own specific elements determined both by the nature of the particular ideas to be represented and by the character of the medium in which it finds expression. In general, it is true that thus envisaged a study of art shows certain characteristic *forms* and relationships between them. Thus architecture has its columns, its arches of various styles, its windows and walls, the dome, the porch, the cornice, etc., structural forms to be variously disposed and arranged; sculpture has the different parts of the human body or of other forms to be designed truly, and to be disposed both accurately and gracefully or significantly. And even literature, that art in which content counts for so much, is by no means barren of formal elements. Mention may be made of such elements as metre, rhythm, rhyme, balance, euphony and the like. Now music, as well as the other arts, has its own characteristic formal and architectonic attributes. Not only so, but in their extreme importance they rank music with architecture, the art of pure form, rather than with literature, the art of deepest thought. This being true, they are evidently worthy of the most careful examination.

It is worthy of notice, also, that in a study of an art for its own sake, attention centres chiefly upon the objective rather than the subjective attribute of that art. Thus, so far as the musician studies his art *technically*, he is engrossed with the formal or structural attributes of the composition examined, rather than with the analysis of the mental reactions it awakens. That this formal side is both rich in its æsthetic possibilities and interesting from an intellectual standpoint, the zeal and enthusiasm of musicians abundantly proves An analysis of a composition, like any other analysis, consists of the separation of a composition into its elements so that their inherent nature can be intelligently understood, and the beauty and significance of their synthesis appreciated. That these musical elements of form must be some series of single tones or chords, possessing in themselves more or less unity and character, follows from the character of music itself.

2. Two main reasons may be given why the subject of Musical Form is vital for a philosophy of this art. In the first place, form is a constituent element in music, and as such plays its own part in the musical experience. Since a work of art must be a concrete, sensuous form, these elements of form are a part of the real artistic reality of the art in question, and as such cannot be disregarded.

In the second place, form in art is important because the thought content is vitally influenced, not to say conditioned by these formal elements. The form of an art is, as it were, the mold into which the art conception is cast, and therefore limits even the thought itself. Form and content are inseparable and for art both indispensable. 'And the form is not only influenced by the content, but the content by the form as well. As Lessing long ago but once for all made plain, only a limited class of ideas is suitable for pictorial representation; while another limited class is the proper subject for expression under the form of literature.

The argument is so terse and so convincing that though well known it is given in the note below.[1] The same principle is involved in the case of music. Its content is determined partly by the medium in which it is expressed, but partly by the forms in which convention has decided musical ideas should be cast. Thus, not only to appreciate music critically as the musician appreciates it, but to understand it philosophically the formal elements must be given their due consideration.

3. The *scale* is of such fundamental importance in music, both from the objective and from the sub-

[1] "I infer thus· If it is true that painting employs in its imitations quite different media or signs from poetry, the former employing shapes and colors in space, the latter articulate tones in time; if it is unquestionable that the signs must have a convenient relation to the thing signified, then coexisting signs can only express objects which coexist or whose parts coexist, and successive signs can only express objects which are successive or whose parts are successive

"Objects which coexist or whose parts coexist are called bodies. Consequently bodies with their visible qualities are the proper objects for painting.

"Objects which are in succession, or whose parts are in succession, are called actions. Consequently actions are the proper objects of poetry."

Quoted from Bosanquet, *History of Æsthetic*, p. 224.

jective points of view, that the principal facts concerning it, even though they are well known, must
be brought to mind anew. Especially is this urgent
for an adequate understanding of the principles of
musical form, the subject which is to engage our
immediate attention.

Under the equal-tempered system of tuning, the
piano keyboard, both in pitch and in compass,
represents substantially our Western musical system. For the sake of simplicity and because it
is the instrument most readily available, our discussion will be in terms of the keyboard of this
instrument. On the seven-octave keyboard there
are eighty-five distinct sounds forming a series and
differing from one another primarily in pitch. The
interval between any two successive sounds in this
series is approximately uniform, the interval being
known as a semitone or, in the language of the musician, a "minor second." If we strike all the keys of
the piano in order, beginning with the lowest or the
highest, we have the complete "chromatic scale,"
and have heard essentially all the sounds (at least
as regards pitch) used in Western music.

But this series of sounds readily breaks up into
definitely related groups which are of fundamental
importance in the musical art. These are the octaves
and the scales. For example, if after striking any
given key, the thirteenth key above it be struck
also, the two sounds will be found to combine harmoniously; the one is an octave above the other
and represents the same note. The significance of
the octave will appear in our discussion of the
scales. We need not, therefore, delay to treat it
further at this point.

If we start at any point in the complete chromatic scale represented by the keyboard, and
ascending omit the 2d, 4th, 7th, 9th and 11th keys,
we would play the 1st, 3d, 5th, 6th, 8th, 10th, and
12th; the 13th will be a replica of the 1st, only an
octave higher. A continuation of this order throughout the length of the keyboard, regarding the 13th
always as the beginning of the order to be repeated,
gives us the complete diatonic scale. But as the
order of intervals in the successive octaves is identical, and each sound an exact octave from the same
step in the adjoining octave, it is sufficient to confine our remarks to the scale as it is found within
the limits of an octave. An examination of the
order of sounds as thus limited will show at once
that the major diatonic scale consists of seven distinct musical sounds leading on the eighth step to
a sound just an octave above the first, the scale
being given, of course, in the ascending order. Of
these seven intervals of the scale within the octave
two consist of one step, that is, a semitone, and five
consist of two steps, or whole tones. The minor
seconds or semitones in this scale always occur between the third and fourth and between the seventh
and eighth, both in ascending and descending. Thus
the major diatonic scale may be regarded as eight
sounds selected out of the thirteen in an octave of
the chromatic scale, the essential point being the
position of the two semitone intervals. Now this
scale serves as the standard of the tonal relationships in melody, although it is always possible for
the musician to introduce any of the sounds omitted
in the diatonic scale as occasion demands. But it
is true, nevertheless, that the major diatonic scale

is the scale on which Western music is based primarily. This is true not alone as music is considered structurally, but subjectively, the scale being the very pole-star of mental reference.

From the above explanation the subject of various scales, or in common parlance, the "keys," is readily understood. A major diatonic scale, it is evident, can be begun on any of the twelve distinct notes of the octave, upon the C, or C♯, D, or D♯, E, or F, etc. Each such scale takes its name from the initial note, in flats or sharps, as the case may be. The essential thing is that the relationship of full tones and semitones as given above should be maintained. The difference between the keys therefore is fundamentally a difference in pitch, the sameness or identity a matter of interval relationships. Thus the relationship of sounds to one another in the scale is the unchanging datum, the standard, as has been said, according to which the mind recognizes and appreciates differences in pitch. This relationship, as referring especially to the key note, is the principle of *tonality* to which we shall have occasion to refer later on. It may be said also that just as within the scale some intervals are more natural than others, so any given key has its related keys into which it modulates most readily.

Thus far the fixity of the relationship of the tones of the scale has been the point kept constantly in view and emphasized as of most importance psychologically considered. But with the chromatic scale, consisting of a series of sounds all separated in pitch by a semitone, it is evident that there is opportunity for a somewhat wide variation upon this point, the same number of steps in the octave being retained.

The fact that the semitone in the major diatonic scale comes between the third and fourth and the seventh and eighth is not a musical necessity, but a convention. There is evidently room for considerable variation from this rule before all the possible permutations are used. The Greeks, as a matter of fact, in their various "modes" did recognize variations in this respect that modern music no longer uses. Of these possible variations from the standard major scale modern usage sanctions but one, the so-called *minor scale*, in which the semitone comes between the second and third and, under varying conditions, between the seventh and eighth, as in the major scale, or between the fifth and sixth. The subject of the minor mode, an important one psychologically, will be taken up for discussion in another connection. For the time being, for the sake of simplicity we shall confine ourselves to the major scale.

In the scale itself some sounds are closer related to the key-note than others, the relationship being capable of expression in mathematical ratios, the basis being the number of vibrations per second made by the individual sounds. Just as among the Twelve Apostles three were found whose hearts were in closer accord than the others to the heart of the Master, so in the twelve tones of the chromatic scale there are three which harmonize best with the key-note. These are the fifth or *dominant*, with a vibrational ratio of 2.3; the fourth or *sub-dominant*, its ratio being $3:4$; and the third or *mediant*, whose ratio is $4:5$. The octave with a relation of $1:2$ is not considered as a separate sound, but as the key-note repeated and strengthened. In music objectively considered, these relationships are of the utmost importance; no small part of harmony is based upon the truth thus simply expressed. But great as is the importance of these relationships from the objective point of view, from the subjective standpoint they are no less fundamental; here their closer relationship to the key-note makes them subjective points of reference, points of rest and recognition in the successive tones of melody or chords of harmony.

The last phrase leads us to another definition, necessary even in this fragmentary outline of musical principles. I refer to the fundamental chord or triad, which can be built up on any one of the twelve tones of the chromatic scale. For example, if any one of these tones is selected and regarded as a key-note and with it is combined its *third* and its *fifth*, we have a chord or harmony which may stand for mental reference in the place of the key-note itself. If, in the same way, a chord is built up upon the *fifth*, taking its *third* and *fifth* we have the *dominant triad* or harmony for the given key. Chords formed in the same way upon *sub-dominant* or upon the *mediant*, form the *sub-dominant* and *mediant triads* respectively. In modern harmonic music these triads or chords serve the purpose of their basic notes in simple melody; that is to say, they serve as points of reference and of rest in music of the ordinary harmonic type. Such are some of the more fundamental facts of musical theory preliminary to a discussion of form proper.

4. It has already been suggested that the elements of musical form, in the nature of the case, must be certain combinations of musical tones having a cer-

tain individuality and unity of their own. In view of this fact the natural point at which to begin a discussion of the structural or formal elements of music is with the *phrase*. By a musical phrase we mean a structural element of melody (which may or may not be harmonized) of two or more measures, and terminated at the completion of a certain number of rhythmic units by some form of cadence. The number of measures in a phrase is variable, two being the minimum, four the most typical number, five, six, or seven not uncommon, eight comparatively frequent, and more not exceptional. Mendelssohn is said to have written a phrase consisting of twenty-two measures. This, however, is exceptional. Manifestly the number of measures the phrase contains is not its determining attribute; neither is the rhythm, for this also is variable. But if not its length or its rhythm, then evidently the cadential termination is the secret of its individuality.

By a *cadence* in music is meant the *falling* (or rising) of the melody at the end of a rhythmic unit to one of the fundamental notes of the scale, to the tonic or to the dominant in most cases.[1] If the phrase ends with the tonic, the cadence is said to be perfect; if with the dominant, it is said to be an imperfect cadence or a half cadence. Interpreted in terms of harmony, which in modern music is all but the universal form, the tonic triad would take the place of the key-note, giving a perfect cadence; the dominant triad the place of the dominant, giving the half cadence. The musician has other distinctions

---

[1] Rhythmic unit is here used to denote nothing more definite than that the cadence must come at the completion of a certain number of measures.

for various other forms of endings, but for our purposes it will be best to let a few of the more fundamental examples suffice. As examples of phrases
we may give the following:

ARNE· "Artaxerxes"

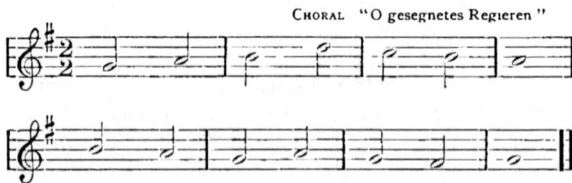

CHORAL "O gesegnetes Regieren"

In the second example there are two phrases each
of four measures, the first, ending at the fourth
measure on a half cadence, the second, as in the
eighth measure, on a perfect or full cadence. But
for simplicity there are no better examples of phrases
than the music corresponding to the various lines in
our familiar songs and hymns.

As calling attention to the importance of the
phrase in music and to certain of its characteristics,
the following words are pertinent: "It is necessary
to emphasize the importance of the phrase, for from
it all musical forms are built, and in all productions
of music, whether instrumental or vocal, the proper
accenting and phrasing is as vital as in the speak-
ing and reading of a language. That the phrase may

NOTE —The shorter quotations in this chapter are taken from
Prout's *Musical Form*, unless otherwise indicated.

be distinguished by the listener it is necessary that
an apparent change be made in the rhythm; this is
brought about by the usual introduction of the
cadence, which is the end of the phrase or the point
of temporary repose between two phrases. The
cadence generally occurs upon an accented beat,
and its presence is commonly made known by the
lengthening of the chord which is sounded at that
point; when this chord is built up from the key-note
of the phrase, the pause is said to be a full cadence;
when the chord is that of the fifth, it indicates a half
or imperfect cadence. The significance of the full
and the half-cadence will be apparent later in this
same chapter. The cadence is commonly very apparent, and rightfully so, as next to the knowledge
of melody, the finding of the true location of the
cadence is the most important task in properly
analyzing and interpreting music; yet in many
cases the cadence is partially concealed by various
technical devices which it is unnecessary to mention
here as we are striving to gain only a general understanding of our subject." [1]

5. Though the phrase in music by virtue of its cadential ending is, subjectively considered, the small-
est fundamental unit, it is not incapable of analysis.
The phrase is usually divided into sections, divisions
determined both by accent or rhythmic, and by pitch
relations. There is no absolute uniformity in the
length of sections, even for any given length of phrase.
Prout's summary states the essential facts "In
many cases, though not invariably, the phrases will
themselves be divided into *Sections*. Though it is

[1] *The American History and Encyclopedia of Music. Theory*, pp.
176–177.

possible for even a section to end with a full cadence,
we mostly find the cadential effect less distinct in a
section than in a phrase. Very often if a sentence
consists of two phrases, one of these will be subdivided into two sections, while the other is indivisible.
By this means variety of detail is obtained without
the sacrifice of symmetry." [1]   For example, the sentence quoted above, given here in its harmonized
form that the cadential effect may be more marked,
is divided into sections as follows:

The shorter brackets here indicate the sections,
the larger the phrases. One other example may be
given.

[1] *Musical Form*, p. 35.

Haydn "Symphony in G"

6. Continuing our analysis of the phrase, we come to another element of music, the *motive*, which structurally is of much greater significance than the section, for it is often used as the basis of what is known as thematic music. As the usual mensural length of the section consisted of two strongly accented notes, that is, ordinarily of two measures, so the usual length of the motive is such as to include one and only one of the primary accents of the measure. Prout's definition will help to make this clear. "A motive is composed of a strongly accented note, preceded by one or more unaccented or less accented notes, and followed by unaccented notes, only when the harmony requires it, or the context shows that the following motive does not begin immediately

after the accent." [1]   The definition calls attention
to the fact that exceptions to the general rule are
possible, and perhaps not uncommon. Into an analysis of such variations from the rule, the purpose of
our discussion does not compel us to enter. It will
be for our purposes sufficient to find the general
truth, the common principles which express not alone
the ruling form, but which determine the exceptions
as well. No rule without its exceptions, we are told,
but certainly, no exceptions without a rule.

The first period of the Choral quoted above is thus
divided into motives:

Each phrase, it will be noticed, begins with an incomplete motive, the others being reducible to the regular or inverted form of the very simple motive of

two notes in the relation .   But one of

the best classic examples of the *motive*, both because
of its inherent individuality and because of the wonderful use made of it, is the *motive* upon which Beethoven has built the first movement of the Symphony
in C minor.

"Such," he said, "is the knock of Fate."   In order

---

[1] *Ibid.*, p. 31.

that the reader may not neglect to hear it anew I quote a few measures.

BEETHOVEN· "Symphony in C Minor."

There are several devices open to the musician by which he is able to develop from a simple motive an orderly and logical artistic whole. Some of these have been exemplified in the music already quoted, and are worthy of a brief notice even in a sketch which purports to be only the briefest possible outline of the element of musical form. In the first place, the motive may be repeated either literally or with certain variations. If repeated literally, that is, without change in pitch or rhythm, its use is obvious. But since the motive consists of two distinct elements, viz., *pitch relationships* and *rhythmic figure*, so to speak, it is possible to modify either the order of the intervals or the rhythmic value of the notes without destroying the identity of the basic motive. For example, the motive is frequently repeated at different points in the scale, the intervals and rhythm being retained, as in the first instance cited; or the rhythm being retained, the intervals may be modified as is done in the Symphony quoted; or subordinate variations may be made in both the intervals and in the time elements without entirely obscuring the identity of the subject. A note or notes may be amplified by substituting two-eighths for a quarter or two quarters for a half, etc.

Inversion is another variation by means of which substantial modifications are introduced. This process consists of using the notes in an inverse order, so that the interval is changed from an ascending order to a descending or *vice versa*, the interval or intervals being retained. Examples of this process are found in the Choral cited above. The device being common, however, the following examples may well be noticed [1]

or the modification of this process in Beethoven's Sonata, Op. 26,

which is repeated as follows:

By such structural devices and others not mentioned, the musician can develop from even the simplest motive a very complex and yet a perfectly logical, artistic whole. For a fuller discussion of this technical subject the reader is referred to musical literature.

Thus far the discussion has been limited to an analytic study of the phrase. But this same structural

[1] Quoted from Cornell's *Musical Form*, pp. 91-92.

unit by synthetic processes enters into the highest
and most complex musical forms, such as the sonata
and the symphony. It is in this rather than in its
own well-marked individuality that its true musical
significance is found.

The musical phrase, notwithstanding the elements
of unity it possesses, as the name itself would indicate, is not able to stand alone and unrelated to other
phrases. Just as in language the phrase is incomplete apart from its use in the sentence, so the musical phrase apart from the balanced *after-phrase* fails
to produce in the mind that sense of finality and rest
which characterizes the expression of a complete
thought. The principle of dual balance is so essential to music that in the larger structural forms it is a
rule almost without exception that every phrase or
combination of phrases must be balanced by a phrase
or combination of phrases of equal temporal value.
The phrase is a unit, but music is a composition of
phrases, and in placing them together order must be
observed. Compare for example, the feeling of unity
and completeness produced by the single phrase and
the period of two balanced phrases following it.

ARNE: "Artaxerxes"

HAYDN: "Symphony in C."

7. The simplest combination of phrases would be
manifestly two phrases of equal length balanced the
one against the other as in the example just quoted
from Haydn. This simple form of two phrases thus
balanced is known among musical theorists as the
sentence or *period*, the latter, perhaps, the more common designation. When two periods in turn are balanced the one against the other, the necessity for
having the *fore-phrase* and the *after-phrase* (as the
two phrases of the period are called) of equal length
is obviated; the demand for symmetry and balance
is met in such a case by the more comprehensive
balance of period against period. The case here is
altogether analogous to balance and symmetry in
architecture. For example, if there are in the façade
of a building but two windows, one on each side of
the central doorway, symmetry demands that they
should be of equal size; but if there are two on each
side of the door, symmetry is maintained if one be
large, one small, provided those on the opposite side,
and in the same order, are of like form. This is the
secret not only of the principle of dual balance but
of the whole formal architectonic of music. Thus, in
the period the cadential feeling at the end of the
phrases is supplemented by the feeling of balance or
symmetry.

In the period the first phrase is usually terminated
by some form of a half cadence, thus pointing on
to the second phrase as the true conclusion of the
musical thought. This psychological effect may
be noticed in the following example, or by running
through, line by line, any of our standard simple
songs.

But even such a symmetrical form as the period
does not furnish sufficient body to serve as a genuine
art form, except in very unusual cases. Just as a single sentence or a paragraph however well turned or
decoratively printed will hardly rank as a work of
literary art, so the period in music, whether composed
of four or eight-measure phrases, will not suffice as
the standard for musical form. It is too fragmental,
however perfect in itself, to merit the noble name of
art. Schumann, it is true, has written a composition
of only eight measures, Op. 79, No. 1, but this is only
an exception that proves the rule.

8. The simplest combination of phrases usually regarded as a standard art form is the simple *Two-Part*,
or *Binary Form;* or, as it is often called, the *Song-
Form.* This form structurally is simplicity itself,
being composed merely of two related periods. Although it is composed frequently of one period
simply repeated, the more usual form is to find
some variation introduced in the fore-phrase of the

¹ Quoted from Cornell's *Musical Form*, p. 28.

second period, the after-phrase of this period being
the same as the after-phrase of the first period. The
following is a typical illustration:

FIRST PERIOD. Beethoven [1]

SECOND PERIOD

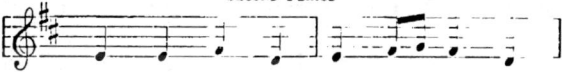

When it is remembered that in this form the length
of the phrases, the melody, the harmony, and the
rhythm are all variable quantities, it is evident that
even in such a simple form as this there is the possibility for much originality and for various styles of
music. The list of musical forms which, when ana-

[1] Quoted from Cornell's *Musical Form*, p 40

lyzed show this simple binary structure, is not small, and the compositions are all but innumerable. First, may be mentioned the great body of hymns, in which there is usually but little variation from the normal form. We give but one familiar one to show the structure.

As the name "Song-Form" suggests, this is also the typical form of most of our common and well-loved songs; indeed, it was given this name from the fact that the Volkslieder of Germany were written in this form. In the list of binary forms, therefore, must be included most of the simple, well-loved songs of the people, such as *Annie Laurie, Blue-bells of Scotland, Old Folks at Home,* and their ilk. In structure they are so simple and their unity is so evident that they are the standard of true music for those who are unable to appreciate the unity of forms of a more complex structure.

Still another important use of this form in music is found in waltzes and other forms of dances, not merely of the popular type, but of the best composers. Schubert, for example, has more than two hun-

dred of his shorter compositions written in this form.
One of them is here given.

SCHUBERT, "Trauer Waltzer," Op 9, No 2.

These few examples will suffice to give the reader
a general idea of this simplest musical form, to show
its extended use, and to illustrate its possibilities as
a simple, logical form. What has been said or shown,
however, will hardly suggest, except to the musician,
all the possibilities for variation, embellishment, and
personal idiosyncrasies which composers have found
opportunity to introduce, even in this extremely
simple form. To do this, however, is beside our
present purpose, and impossible within the limita-
tion of the chapter to be devoted to this subject.
All that can be done is again to refer the reader to
treatises on this subject.

9. The other typical musical form is the *Three-
Part* or *Ternary* Form. Though a little more complex, it, too, in its plan is so simple that its logical
structure can be understood by any one. Instead of
the two related periods or sentences of the binary
form simply, there is first a complete binary form
ended by a full cadence in the tonic key; the second
part, often in another key, and contrasted with the
first also by the use of new subject matter, may be
a complete binary form, though often it will modu-
late back to the original key instead of closing with
a cadence in the key in which it is written; the

third part is a repetition of the first part simply,
that is, without variations; or changes of minor
importance may be introduced. Frequently a *coda*
or tail-piece is added. A single example is given
with the parts marked respectively I, II, and III.

Andante. BEETHOVEN: "Sonatina," Op 79.

(II)

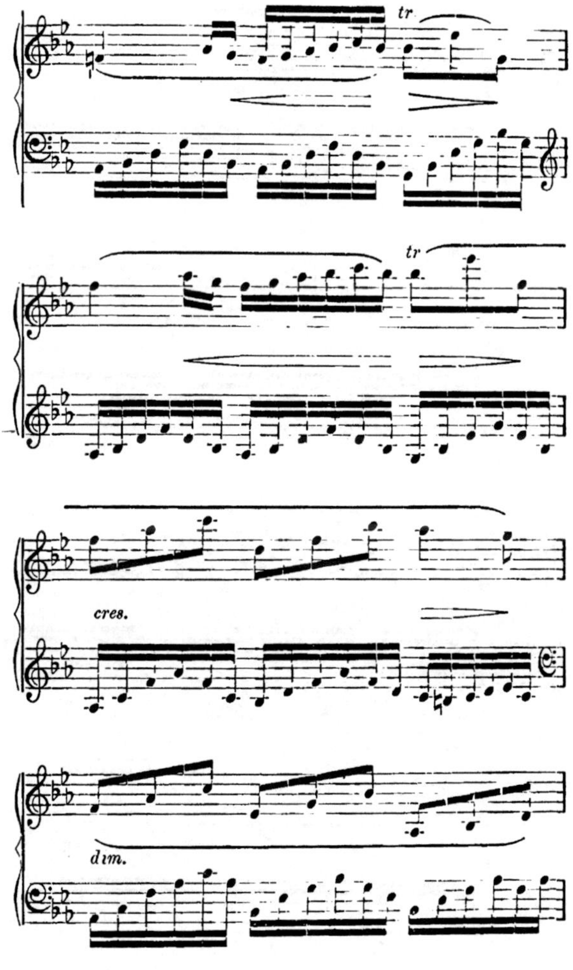
tr
tr
cres.
dim.

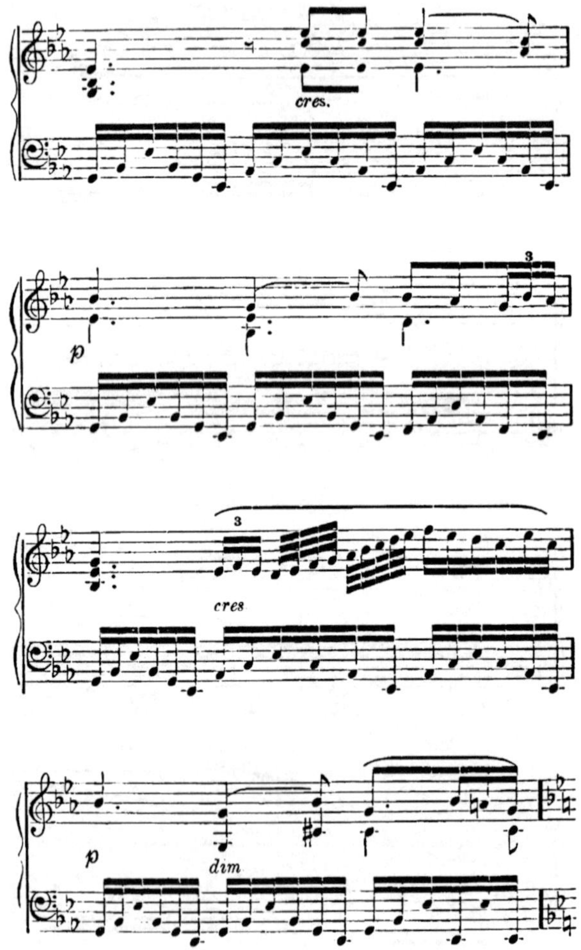
cres.
p
cres
p
dim

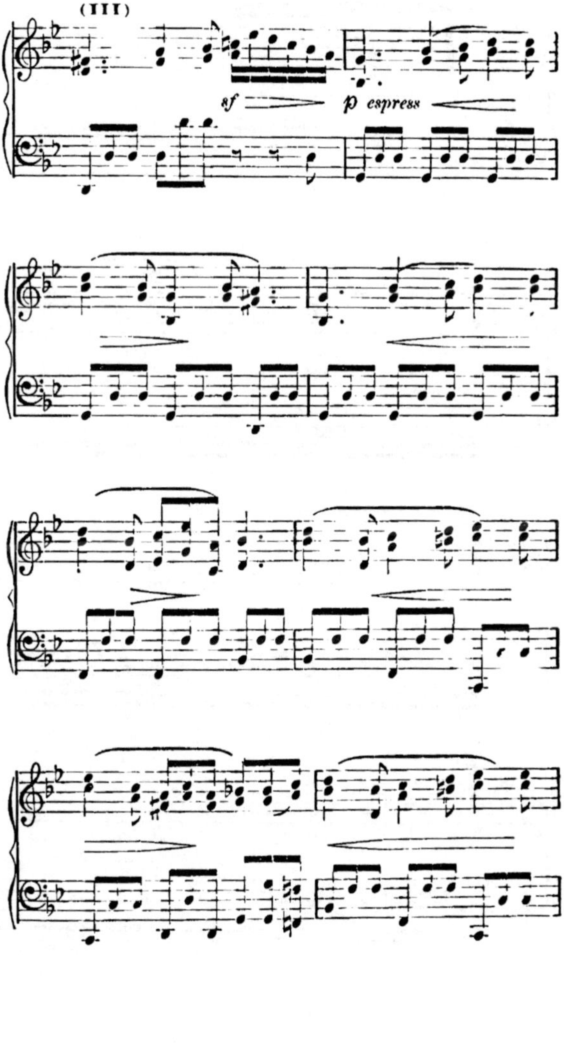
(III)
sf
p espress

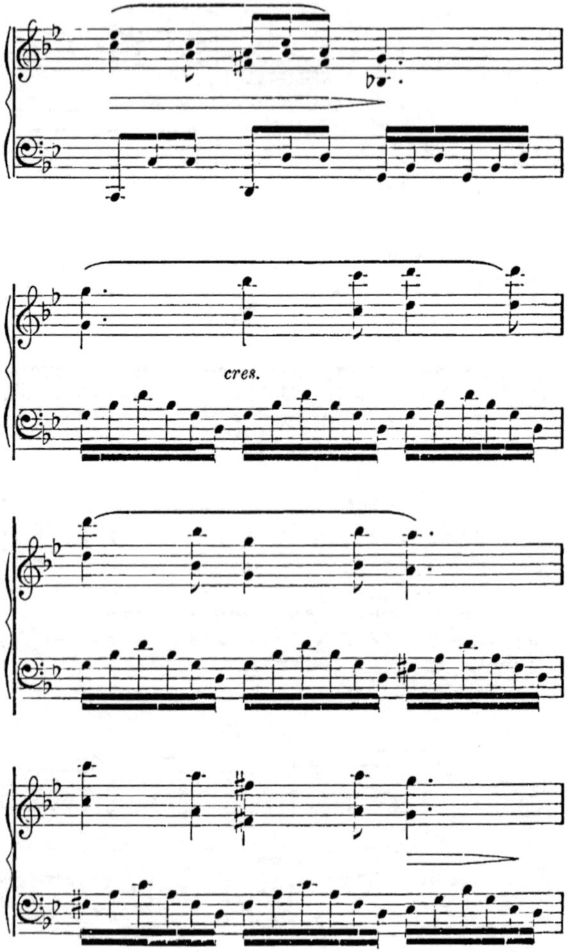
cres.

The following is Prout's analysis of this movement: "The first part of the movement (to the end
of bar 8) is a complete binary form containing two
sentences, the first closing in the relative major and
the second returning to the tonic key. The second
part of the movement begins with a modulation to
E flat, in which key we find the episode. This is
also made of two sentences; the first is four bars in
length, ending with a full close (bar 4), with feminine ending; the second sentence is extended to
five bars by the repetition of its first bar an octave
higher. Its fore-phrase finishes with an interrupted
cadence (bar 6), and its after-phrase with a full
cadence in bar 8. The second part is completed by
a third sentence, modulating back to G minor and
ending with a half cadence in that key. The third
part is an exact repetition of the first, followed by
a coda of one sentence in which four bars are extended to five by the sequential repetition of the
second bar. The final cadence has a feminine
ending."[1]

The ternary form is found both in the larger
compositions of the leading composers, in sonatas,
symphonies, and quartets, in the slow movements,
the minuets, and scherzos, and in many composi-

[1] *Musical Form*, p. 188.

tions written for the piano such as nocturnes, impromptus, etc. This form, like the binary, is subject to the widest possible variation in its rhythmic, melodic, and harmonic structure, so that only the trained musician is able to appreciate intellectually many of the finer structural points which make music, not only a subject worthy of the most careful study, but the medium of expression for true genius, and the most varied forms of individuality. All of this, however, in the present discussion has been left untouched that attention may be concentrated upon the basic principles of musical form and of structural unity in the various forms of musical compositions. To go into a detailed examination of all the modifications of these principles and forms is the proper work of the musician, not of the student of philosophy. It must suffice in the present connection if we have gained some knowledge of musical terminology, have learned the language of the country, as it were, and have shown that music as well as the other arts has its proper basis of unity in certain definite structural forms.

PART II

THE PSYCHOLOGICAL ANALYSIS
OF MUSIC

CHAPTER III

RHYTHM

1. An analysis of a musical composition shows three distinct elements in modern music—Rhythm, Melody, and Harmony.[1] Whatever the type of the composition, however strong the personal equation of the composer, every composition worthy of serious consideration will show these factors coalesced to form a complete and unitary work of art. These three elements, therefore, serve as the natural basis for our psychological analysis of music. What is the essential nature of each, and, more important, what is the nature of the psychological reaction to which each gives rise? The answer to these two questions will give us the data upon which to base conclusions as to the true philosophical character of music and of its relations to other forms of human experience.

So many scientific investigations of rhythm have been made that it may seem both useless and presumptuous to attempt to add anything to what is already known and has been frequently repeated. Herbert Spencer, for example, has treated the subject in its cosmic relations and shown its presence

[1] In the light of the stress now being laid upon orchestration, it is an open question whether *color* should not be added to this trinity of elements. But as what is known as color introduces no new psychological element in the musical experience, we shall confine our discussion in the main to the three elements mentioned.

57

and significance as a law of motion in the evolution of the material world. Its adaptability to the method of physiological and psycho-physical research has made it a favorite subject for experimental investigation in our laboratories, and its importance as an element in music has led the musical fraternity to analyze it as a factor in music. But notwithstanding all that has been done along these various lines the inquiry we propose has not been explicitly answered. The principal facts concerning rhythm, it may be, have been ascertained, but the argument to prove our point has not been formulated. Thus there is abundant reason why we must take up the subject anew, treat it in our own way, and justify our conclusions by our own arguments. That so much matter is available makes the task easier, but it does not obviate the need for undertaking it.

2. Genetically considered, rhythm is the primary factor from which music as well as dancing and poetry have developed; it is the dynamic that first aroused the mind to an instinct or desire for artistic expression. Parry, it is true, makes the rhythmic and the melodic factors coördinate, but he does this in a general way without raising the question of the real temporal primacy of either of the two.[1] Upon the basis of physiological and biological investigations rhythm must be accorded the honor of antiquity and regarded as the root from which have developed the various attempts of primitive men for artistic expression. It is, of the three elements of music, unquestionably the one deepest seated in the human organism, and biologically can be traced

[1] *Vid. Evolution of the Art of Music*, Ch. I.

lower down in the scale of life than our susceptibility for either melodic or harmonic factors. As it
is found in man susceptibility to rhythm is an
instinct, and he responds to it reflexly and almost
inevitably; it seems, therefore, to be fixed in the
very heart of that most vital of all vital substances,
the nervous system. In modern anthropological
and genetically psychological investigations rhythm
looms large. G. Stanley Hall says: "In the dark
background of history there is now much evidence
that at some point play, art, and work were not
divorced; they may all have sprung from rhythmic
movement, which is so deep-rooted in biology because it secures most joy of life with least expense." [1]
But stronger, more positive still, are the words of
Karl Bucher, who says. "In that centre of conver-
gence we see work still undistinguished from art and
from play. There is a single human activity, a
solution of work, play and art. In this unity of
physical and mental activity we perceive the germs
of development all along these lines. . . . The arts
of motion, music, dance, and poetry came into being
in the performance of work; the arts of rest of form
are embodied, if only in the forms of movement, in
the results of work. This is all simply the instinctive action of life in common average humanity
in savages, in peasants, in working people. The
bond that holds together these elements which we
have come to think so unlike is rhythm, whose
source is in the very essence of the human organism." [2]

Further probability of the correctness of this

[1] *Adolescence*, Vol. I, p. 211.
[2] *Arbeit und Rhythmus*, p. 357 (quoted from Goodell).

view of the primacy of rhythm is furnished by the wide, almost universal field in which rhythm is found. Not only is rhythm an instinct which functions in the arts, as in music and dancing and poetry, but it is a principle which seems to extend over the whole realm of human activities, both voluntary and involuntary. Mention may be made of the regular systole and diastole of the heart, the periodic recurrence of inspiration and expiration, the longer rhythm of working and sleeping, the recurrence of hunger, the activity of certain glands, the periodic activity of the reproductive organs, the rhythm of walking and of talking, and of thinking as well; the more obscure but no less certain changes connected with the nutrition of the individual cells of the body and even with the growth of the embryo. Considering the wide range of vital processes in which rhythm shows itself as a characteristic attribute, it seems safe to venture the generalization that rhythm is a characteristic of all organic action, though it may be modified by forces we do not as yet understand.

3. To trace all of these various forms of rhythmic action, with the exception of the more obscure forms in nutrition and in the growth of the embryo back to fluctuations in the nervous discharge controlling such actions, is a short step and one that must be taken.

The words of Professor Ladd express a truth to which few psychologists will wish to dissent: "All feelings, as such, but especially as 'pleasure-pains,' are subject to the law of Rhythm and Repetition. The ground for both of these laws is found in the most fundamental conditions of the life and activity of the nervous system itself."[1]   Rhythm, therefore, we conclude is organic, an inherent property of the nervous system, and manifests itself therefore even in the activity of the higher centres with which mental life is so intimately correlated.

That rhythm is a phenomenon connected primarily with the functioning of the nervous system is a fact that goes far toward explaining some of the problems connected with a philosophy of music. Being organic and natural, not a cultivated reaction, it is readily seen why music with a pronounced

[1] Ladd, *Psychology Descriptive and Explanatory*, p 203

NOTE —The physiological explanation of rhythmic discharge of nerve centres is so simple, so illuminating, that it is given in the words of a well-known physiologist

"Suppose a tube closed water-tight below by a hinged bottom, which is kept closed by a spring. If a steady stream of water is poured into the tube from above, the water will rise until its weight is able to overcome the pressure of the spring, and the bottom will then be forced down and some water flow out. The spring will then press the bottom up again, and the water will accumulate until its weight again forces open the bottom of the tube, and there is another outrush, and so on. By opposing a certain resistance to the exit we could thus turn a steady inflow into a rhythmic outflow Or, take the case of a tube with an end immersed in water and a steady stream of air blown into its other end The air will emerge from the immersed end, not in a steady current, but in a series of bubbles Its pressure in the tube must rise until it is able to overcome the cohesive force of the water, and then a bubble bursts forth; after this the air has again to get up the requisite pressure in the tube before another bubble is ejected, and so the continuous supply is transformed into an intermittent delivery Physiologists suppose something of the same kind to occur in the respiratory centre. Its nerve cells are always, under usual circumstances, being excited; but, to discharge a nervous impulse along the efferent respiratory nerves, they have to overcome a certain resistance The nervous impulses have to accumulate, or 'gain a head,' before they travel out from the centre, and, after their discharge, time is required to attain once more the necessary level of irruption before a fresh innervation is sent to the muscles."—Martin's *Human Body*, p 418

accent and strong rhythm finds almost a universal appreciation among mankind. Response to a rythmic stimulus is instinctive, and as inevitable as any other reflex act; it is mechanical, not intellectual or appreciative.

Again, the peculiar power which music with a strongly marked rhythm has for the natural, untutored ear, finds in this physiological theory of rhythm a ready explanation. It is of the nature of physiological reflexes and instincts that they should be clamant, impellant, gaining their end by the mere force of direct impulse rather than by any conscious appreciation of the end to be realized by such action. Consequently such incentives to action are so direct, so powerful indeed in their incitation, that they can be resisted only by the most direct act of will or by a taste for something higher cultivated by long and arduous labor.

4 But the question of supreme importance for a philosophy of music is to determine the nature of the mental response these elements of music elicit. The musical experience is fundamentally a mental, not a physiological phenomenon, and in the end all terms must be reduced to terms of consciousness Hence it will not suffice to regard rhythm merely as a property of nerve activity; its influence upon consciousness is the salient point in the matter.

There are two lines of investigation by which light may be thrown upon the psychological significance of musical rhythm, and, because the subject for musical æsthetics is of paramount importance, neither of them can safely be neglected. The first is an empirical inquiry into the mental effect of musical rhythm as it is found in various types of music. The second method is to carry our psychological analysis of rhythm a step farther and inquire how the rhythmic action of the nervous system manifests itself in consciousness.

In brief, the thesis which we shall endeavor to substantiate is that the natural instinctive effect of rhythm is an *emotional* modification of consciousness. Whatever the possibilities may be for a refined development of this element in music, and for its more intellectual utility as an element in the highest forms of musical composition, the whole weight of evidence genetically considered goes to prove that the emotional is the primary effect upon consciousness. If this be true, as we believe the investigation will clearly prove, it is safe to conclude that, notwithstanding the later more artistic development of rhythm, it never gets away from its primal character or ceases to modify the emotional tone of the conscious state into which it enters. Thus there is found the basis for an emotional element in music which both biologically and psychologically is fundamental and cannot therefore be either denied or disregarded.

5. Rhythm, as has been said, is an attribute of neural activity inbred in the nervous tissue through ages and cycles of development and growth before the mind was capable of true creative work such as both melody and harmony imply. Consequently the music of undeveloped tribes and of uncultivated taste is preponderatingly rhythmical. Instruments of percussion are the favorite musical instruments of men in the lowest stages of mental development. This simple, though strongly reiterated rhythm in monotone is the music of primitive tribes even to-day.

Among such people the almost universal use of the rude drum in war-dances and in ceremonials bespeaks the prevalence of rhythm as the element of music most appreciated, and the results obtained abundantly emphasize its power and indicate in no uncertain way its natural effect upon the human mind. In the war-dance, for example, of our American Indians, we may note its intense emotional power in this crude form; the dance begins with rhythmic movements, accentuated by the beat of a drum, and often accompanied by the repetition of some simple melodic phrase. The phrase, however, serves to do little more than to help mark the rhythm and to give opportunity for a more general expression of rhythmic action. As the tempo is increased the movements of the dancers are accelerated and the emotions raised to higher and higher pitch. This is continued until the minds of those participating in the dance are worked into a fine frenzy and the time for rash counsel and deeds of violence is ripe. Our frontier soldiers of the last century well knew the extent and the dangers of such emotional intoxication. As Parry says, "Pure, unalloyed rhythmic music is found in most parts of the uncivilized globe; and the degree of excitement to which it can give rise, when the mere beating of the drum or tom-tom is accompanied by dancing, is well known to all the world."[1]

In such rhythmic action it is evident that there are none of the finer elements of purely æsthetic emotion: it is little more than an emotional orgy secured by taking advantage of the natural susceptibility of man for rhythmic stimulation. The response is reflex and sensuous, though it contains within it the

[1] *Evolution of the Art of Music*, p. 7.

possibilities for refinement and for true æsthetic reaction.

Mr. Bolton, in his study of Rhythm, says:

"There is no more striking fact in the whole field of
rhythm than the emotional effect which rhythms produce
upon certain classes of people, savages and children. Attention has already been called to the psychological phenomenon of accompanying the changes of intensity in a
series of sounds by muscular movements. So strong is
this impulse in all classes of people that no one is able to
listen to music in which the rhythm is strong and clear
without making some kind of muscular movement. With
some people these movements tend to increase in force
until the whole body becomes involved and moves with the
rhythm. The accents in the rhythm have the effects of
summated stimuli, and the excitement may increase even
to a state of ecstasy and catalepsy. Although the regular
recurrence of the accented syllable is the most important
element, the qualitative changes aid in bringing about the
emotional states. Soothing effects result from certain
rhythms, as is shown in the lulling and patting of a baby
to sleep. The early hypnotizers resorted to the gentle
stroking of their subjects. Savages are well aware of the
exciting effects of certain rhythms, and are accustomed to
use them to bring about the state of frenzy in which their
priests give their prophecies and in which religious dances
are danced. Mr. Ellis, who has made a study of some
tribes in Africa, says, 'Music among the Thsi-speaking
tribes is limited to airs possessing an obvious rhythm.
Such airs seem to appeal to the primitive sense common
to all people, but upon savages, that is, upon children with
the possession and power of men, its influence is immense,
and the state of excitement into which an assemblage of
uncivilized people may be wrought by the mere rhythm of
drums and the repetition of a simple melody, would hardly
be credited. . . . With some races this known emo-

tional influence of music has been utilized with three objects, viz , to stimulate the religious sentiments, the martial spirit, and the sexual passions.'

"In the Yatiati dance among the Indians of British Columbia, the tribe assembles outside of the chief's house in which the dance is to be held, and with fists and sticks they beat the time on the walls as they enter, singing the dancing song. The dancers who are on the inside are worked up into a frenzy. The gentle striking at first, gradually increasing in violence, and the slow approach and the assemblage of the tribe, wrought in the dancers a pitch of excitement which forced them to rush out after a time and begin the dance, jumping about in the wildest fashion. Such dances cease only with the complete exhaustion of the dancers." [1]

In the same article attention is called also to the deep effect upon children of the jingles of childhood. The conclusion to which the author comes is that rhythm among both savages and children is capable of exciting them emotionally, even in some cases to the point of terror or of intoxication. Cases similar to the ones cited might be multiplied indefinitely, for the same emotional excitement under the influence of a strongly accented rhythm is found among all primitive and uncultured people.

The inference to be drawn from such examples is manifest the primary and natural effect of rhythm upon the human mind is directly and dominantly emotional. So close is the relation between nerve action and mental states that, though organic in its causal relations, it manifests itself in consciousness in the most demonstrative and powerful manner. This reaction, in these more primitive

[1] *The American Journal of Psychology*, Jan., 1894, p. 163.

cases is unmistakably and intensely emotional. Such is the conclusion which reference to primitive conditions forces upon us. The further question now arises, whether rhythm throughout the long process of musical development and in the various classes of music recognized to-day retains this emotional power and significance. Reference to certain well-distinguished classes of modern music will readily furnish an answer to this inquiry.

6. In that great body of modern music—waltzes, marches, quicksteps, ballads, rag-time—known collectively as "popular music," rhythm is constructively and psychologically a dominant factor. While such compositions may not be altogether barren of certain minor melodic and harmonic virtues, the real source of their popularity is found in their regular and strongly accented rhythm. Melody and harmony, as will appear later, are the real intellectual elements in music and so, wherever found, require some degree of mental activity for their appreciation; but rhythm, as we have already shown, has an instinctive basis, and reaction to this form of musical stimulus is reflex, as it were, and hence independent of any appreciation of its nature or significance. We shall return to this point, however, in later chapters. The question now at issue is, does this strong rhythmic element in popular music retain recognizable marks of its ancestral character and still exert an unmistakable influence over the emotions?

In answer to this question we notice in the first place the uniformity of the rhythm in such music. As was stated in the last chapter, the rhythm of the phrases is almost without variation, these simpler forms being almost all perfectly normal in their structure. Then, also, the tempo in simple dance music and songs of such form is generally uniformly sustained. In this there is kinship, to say the least, with the more primitive forms of music of undeveloped races. And the psychological effect, though modified by the introduction of other factors, is too evident to be misunderstood.

In martial music, while some of the inspiriting effect must doubtless be attributed to the character of the instruments used, to the *tone color*, it is the strong, stirring rhythm that forms the principal and unvarying characteristic of such music. When the music is accompanied by words, they also must be recognized as having a part in the total effect produced. But they are not essential, as all instrumental music shows. Though the melody in music of this character may differ, and the harmony be good or poor, the rhythm, if strongly accented, and of the proper sort, will almost suffice alone to produce the characteristic reaction. Certain it is that after all proper allowances are made for the effect of words, melody, and harmonization, there remains enough left over to justify us in attributing to rhythm the characteristic quality which belongs to music of this sort. Rhythm not only retains, but it exerts its pristine qualities, moving the spirit in a direct and powerful way to a reaction that is inherently emotional. Witness such stirring hymns as *La Marseillaise* or *Die Wacht am Rhein;* or the effect of the less majestic but no less powerful song of the South, *Dixie.* Often has the writer heard it played in its own sunny land, and seen the remarkable effect upon the audience. As the tempo is increased, so grows the excitement of the listeners, until at the climax, shouts may be heard and hats seen in mid air. This effect is due primarily to the strong rhythm and to the exhilarating tempo for which this air is justly notorious.

Of the same general character are the simple waltzes and "two-steps" which form the major share of the *repertoire* of amateur bands and of musical neophytes. Their popularity is due in part to their structural simplicity, but also largely to the rhythm to which response is made instinctively. That the mental response is emotional, not intellectual, is evident from the ease with which response is made and from the nature of the physical expression of the mental state to which such music gives rise.

When mentioning examples of strong rhythm in popular music, reference must be made also to that peculiar syncopated rhythm known as "rag-time." The rhythm of this music is so characteristic and the effect so evident that it serves as one of the most striking examples of rhythm in popular music. Let the melody be as "catchy" as you please and the harmonization as rich as possible, the force of the rhythmic element will still overshadow them both. *Rag-time*—the name itself indicates its principal characteristic and the source of its power.

That the psychological effect of the rhythm in these examples of popular music and even in martial music of the best sort is essentially of the same nature as in the cruder cases mentioned above, there is no reason to doubt. If the rhythm is strongly accented and the tempo is quick there is the same heightening of the emotional state of consciousness, the same increased excitement and stimulation that the more purely rhythmic music had upon the savage. The stimulus is the same though veiled beneath some melodic and harmonic factors, and the nervous system still is sensitive to such stimulus; the effect, therefore, must be like in kind though somewhat restrained by the conventionalities of an older civilization. It will probably be objected by some whose idols are thus dethroned that there is the greatest difference between the music of savages and popular music to-day. That we would not deny· all that we are here contending for is that the so-called popular music makes great use of rhythm, depends greatly upon it, and that the psychological effect of rhythm upon the mind is still as it has always been. This constant and invariable effect, constant and invariable because natural and instinctive, is an emotional modification of consciousness. And the more marked the rhythm the more pronounced the result until such a time as man, through training and education, has supplanted this instinctive reaction by a desire for, and appreciation of, more intellectual elements. If the race has developed from crude and unrefined reactions to rhythm, to possibilities for appreciating the rhythm of Milton's poetry or of Beethoven's music, so each individual must begin low in the scale of natural reactions to instinctive elements; but he, too, may rise to an appreciation of the greatest masterpieces of poetical or of musical thought.

7. All music, however, is not of this lower order, in which rhythm is psychologically of paramount importance Nor are the purposes of a philosophy of music centred in a discussion of these lower forms of music, but in the highest. The real problem, therefore, the true end of all our seeking, is to determine

the function and value of rhythm in the highest, most artistic forms of music. The modifications of rhythm in music to-day, however, are manifold: reference to some typical uses, therefore, will have to serve our present purpose.

It is a matter of common knowledge that in our highest musical forms, the sonata and the symphony, the division into parts is based upon the *tempo*. Thus in these forms there are such *movements* (notice the term) as the *Allegro*, the *Andante*, the *Largo*, the *Scherzo*, the *Minuetto*, etc. Is the characteristic effect of these different movements due to the rhythm, and if so, just what is the nature of that effect upon consciousness? Or, in the light of what has been determined already, is the psychological effect of the different rhythms in such compositions still emotional, though now more refined and made less obtrusive by the greater importance of melodic and harmonic elements? This question goes deep into the problem, for upon the answer given rests to a large extent the problem of the presence and value of the emotional element in music.

What has been stated concerning the effect of rhythm in the lower forms of music gives the correct answer to the question; it only remains to justify it by showing a little more explicitly that the natural, impressive effect of these *movements* is emotional, that rhythm, even to the limits of its development, is still true to its genesis. In such forms it may lie hidden, as it were, under a wealth of melodic and harmonic elements which charm the sense and claim the active, analytic attention of the mind, and which are the real sources of the artistic value of the composition; but the rhythmic factor is still present, though not obtrusive, and it determines the mood or emotional tone of consciousness that serves as a background upon which the more intellectual elements of melody and harmony stand out in bolder relief. The natural, impressive psychological effect of one of these movements, due chiefly to the rhythm, is a certain emotional state of consciousness, a mood which colors in sombre hues or bright the whole field of consciousness, both focus and fringe. How subtle, but how certain and how powerful is the change when one movement ends and another begins! How few notes it takes to bring the responsive mind from the firm confident mood of an *Allegro* to the more serious, more intense mood of the *Largo!* Or how the shadows lift from their brooding and the sunlight sparkles on leaf and water when the orchestra passes to the *Scherzo!* It is the mood that changes, the emotions that are vaguely but certainly aroused, the facile, affective qualities of mind that respond to the changing stimulus. The suddenness of the change, the directness with which effect follows cause, the quick response the mind gives to the changed music, all reveal the instinctive, the reflex character of the response. This irresistible effect is due not to melodic elements, for it is common to movements notwithstanding the greatest differences in melody, and may come before a single melodic phrase is completed; nor is it due primarily to harmonic features, though it may be emphasized by this means, for again the general effect of a movement is the same under the widest possible differences in harmonic character. There remains, therefore, only the rhythmic element to which we must attribute this striking impressive effect of the different movements.

To make clear by illustration what has been stated abstractly, the reader is asked to listen to such contrasted movements as are represented in the following brief selections taken from Beethoven's Sonatas.

Allegro vivace

Op 2, No 2.

ADAGIO, from Op. 2. No. 1.

SCHERZO, from Op 26

ANDANTE, from Op 26.

These are but a few examples to illustrate what all
music shows. Each composition, if lyrical, engenders
some mood which rises, is lived, and gives place
to some other emotional state as attention passes
to some other of the thousand forms of stimuli to
which the mind is sensitive; each composition of the
more complex sort, like the sonata or the symphony,
by the changed rhythm of the various movements,
and by the corresponding play of melody and force
of harmony, leads us on from one emotional state to
another, the total experience being bound together
by the artistic unity of the composition considered as
a whole. Not that this is the whole of the musical
experience by any means, but for him who enters ap-
preciatively into the spirit of the music this part is
certainly essential.

In literature the affective state is determined by the imagery the words call forth and by the working out of the plot, whether in comedy or tragedy, to living joy and light, or to sorrow and death. Milton's *Lycidas*, for example, is filled with the solemnity of life, gained by the imagery called forth by his wonderfully chosen words. Music gains the same end, produces the same effect, but in an entirely different way. Instead of appealing to the mind by pictures of sorrow or by definite thoughts concerning the solemnities of life, music casts its spell in a more direct way by appealing to an old and instinctive mode of reaction.

Thus, rhythm is the natural basis for an emotional interpretation of music which, though not the final word in musical theory, is the first and as such must be carefully weighed in making up the final verdict. This does not at all preclude the possibility of its having an important function in other directions, but it does suggest that it can never outgrow or escape this influence over the emotions. Being ingrained in the nervous system it may be turned to intellectual purposes, but it can never lay aside its birthright, nor in one generation obliterate all traces of its genetic origin and use.

8. The emotional effect of rhythm is further substantiated by a psychological analysis of rhythm. It must be confessed, however, that there is still so little known concerning the physical basis of the emotional life that it is at present impossible to go very far in this direction or to speak with any great assurance. Consequently, theory and hypothesis must often be given to supply lacunæ in scientific knowledge. However, what is thought or believed may be

given not as proof, but as evidence corroborating the results of the empirical method. As such it has, if not demonstrative, at least some cumulative strength.

There is a physiological theory of the emotional aspect of consciousness which holds that the normal, healthful, functional activity of any organ is accompanied with a pleasurable concomitant in consciousness. With an increased activity of the organ up to a maximum there is an increase in the pleasure resulting therefrom. This point of greatest pleasure is the point where the destructive or katabolic changes exceed to a certain degree the restorative or anabolic processes in the organ involved, and in the nerve centres controlling such organs.

In music a quick tempo well marked tends to increase the activity of these centres and so produces a feeling of life and of exhilaration distinctly pleasurable. The vital functions under a rhythmic stimulus are augmented and the feeling tone rises as a consequence. If the rhythm is sufficiently impressive, this reflex response may so overshadow all else that the character of the response as a whole is determined more by this than by the other musical elements. In the same way the rhythm of a slow tempo tends to retard the physiological processes in the nerve centres and so to produce in consciousness the feeling tone of a lowered or hindered vitality. Thus we have the two general classes of emotions, the excitatory and the serious, the exhilarating and the calm, due, according to this theory, to the physiological effect of a rhythmic stimulus upon the nerve centres.

The ultimate physiological explanation of these changes within the nerve centres is not known. Further attempts to understand the matter would lead us into the realm of biological and evolutional hypotheses.

A hypothesis that in some ways better meets the conditions than this purely physiological theory is that by a uniform and long-continued connection the bodily reaction and the emotion are so closely associated that they have become interchangeable as cause and effect. That is to say, the physiological changes produce emotional modifications of consciousness, but the emotions also have power to produce characteristic changes in the bodily organism. Thus when the listener hears a well-accented rhythm his body attunes itself, it may be reflexly, to the given rate of nervous discharge, and the appropriate mood or feeling state spreads over consciousness; or, on the other hand, the emotion being present, centrally stimulated it may be, the sensitive organism at once adjusts itself by the proper motor changes to the new phase of feeling. Sorrow or grief, or the emotions aroused by the contemplation of the more serious problems of life, produce a lowered vitality, a retardation of the nervous discharges and a palpable inhibition in the intellectual processes; on the other hand, joy, gladness, humor, or the excitement of good news, raises the general tone of the system, and quickens and strengthens the activity of the various centres, both motor and conscious.

While there would be the greatest difficulty encountered in an attempt to formulate the rules for the bodily expression of all emotional nuances, the general principle involved comports well with the emotional theory of the psychological significance of rhythm. Thus the psychological argument, while inadequate in itself, confirms the historical and we are forced to the conclusion that the natural, instinctive effect of rhythm is emotional; and further, that even to the highest point of its artistic development it never loses its fundamental psychological character or is false to its origin.

CHAPTER IV

RHYTHM (*Continued*)

1. It has been suggested more than once in the last chapter that there is, besides the emotional characteristics of rhythm there considered, another aspect to the subject, the consideration of which was only postponed, not disregarded. The time has come now to turn to this neglected phase of the subject and to consider rhythm in its more definitely intellectual relationships. Primitive music, it was said, is primarily and predominantly rhythmical, and the mental response it elicits from the hearer is crudely but intensely emotional. This, however, is but the starting-point; before the end is reached it is quite possible that new factors then undreamed of may enter, and that the mental response may be so modified as to seem almost to lose its kinship with the primitive form of reaction. Radical changes have in truth taken place as music has developed. While the emotional element is never lost, new factors have been introduced, and even the more primitive elements have been so modified that the account of music as then known and used is no longer adequate or complete.

This development of music has been in the direction of greater refinement in its emotional elements, and toward the introduction and greater use of intellectual constituents. The first line of progress has

been briefly sketched in the last chapter. The other movement is not less characteristic or significant. It is seen primarily in the increased importance given to melody and harmony, a movement yet to be discussed, but also in the development of rhythm so as to demand no little intellectual activity for its apprehension and appreciation.

2. As indicative of an intellectual, rather than an emotional character, we would call attention first to the mathematical foundation and exactitude of rhythm. In musical rhythm we have an element in this art that must conform to the strictest requirements of mathematical relations. So unusual is this in art, so suggestive of the intellectual rather than the emotional, that on the face of things it would seem to have some significance certainly for a philosophy of music. There is also such a well-defined tendency in music of recent years to make use of these mathematical relationships that we cannot dismiss the subject without a few words to emphasize this truth. Gurney thus calls attention to the principle of dual balance in music: "There is, however, one fundamental characteristic of rhythm, especially marked in the superior musical development of man, which may, I think, be accounted for on grounds which take us back to primeval times; namely, the characteristic of *dual balance*. As soon as any differentiation at all supervenes on a simple series of equidistant accents, as soon, that is, as such a series is divided off into parts, felt as having a beginning and an end, the principle on which these parts are formed is multiplication by two; . . . To put it in another way, any complete melodic phrase stops after two, or four, or six component bars, and so on, but not after

one, or three, or five. A component phrase may consist of an uneven number of bars, as three or five; but
it will be answered by another of three or five. Nor
must this be understood merely of melodies and subjects which can be reasonably presented alone; it applies to clause after clause in the longest and most
elaborate paragraphs, bar answering bar, and pair of
bars answering pair of bars, though linked into a
series from which no independent bits could be detached."[1]

This, however, is only the beginning of the complex simplicity of rhythm. It is within the bar itself
that we begin to realize the real mathematical character of rhythm, and to see the possibilities for rhythmic
variation in the treatment of a theme or subject and
its development. To show this I can do no better
than quote another paragraph from the work just
mentioned. In this paragraph, summed up in a mar-
ginal note as the "main facts of musical rhythms,"
he says: "It will readily be understood that the complexities of rhythm in Music are not only not incom-
patible with the simple regularity of the main rhythmic basis, but are really only possible through its
existence. The spaces of time during which any note
in a musical paragraph lasts, and the intervals of time
or *rests* often intervening between the end of one note
and the beginning of another, are proper fractions,
usually quite simple ratios, of a constant standard;
and this standard is the length of the bar—that is,
the length of time between two main accents, in relation to which every other time-length is estimated,
and without which a variety of time-lengths would
be perfectly vague and unintelligible. But though

[1] *Power of Sound*, pp 132–133.

the ordinary subdivision of the bar by multiples of two and three makes the fractions as a rule tolerably simple, yet as, e. g., one note may last for a whole bar and another for only the sixty-fourth part of a bar, we shall not soon exhaust the possible arrangements. Thus, not to take an extreme case, $\frac{15}{32}$, $\frac{1}{2}$, $\frac{16}{32}$, are the ratios which the three notes sounded in this

bar bear to the whole length

of the bar, and as the $\frac{15}{32}$ and $\frac{16}{32}$ could each be divided up in any number of ways which would retain 32 as the denominator of the component fractions, while each unit of the division may be represented either by a sound or a silence, the range of subdivision is clearly wide enough for a bar's length to give scope for an endless number of combinations; and every bar of a series may differ in its internal time-arrangements from every other. Such is the possible variety, that it scarcely occurs to one to call either the bars or any of the subordinate groups by the name of *feet*, which would seem to imply that the various sorts could be numbered and catalogued: at the outside, one would apply such a term to a few very simple and common examples. Thus *complete* musical rhythms—complete series of time-relations—are not fixed and general things, like recognized poetical metres, but infinitely various. The great distinction between one musical rhythm and another has no reference to these endless combinations, but to rhythmical *outlines*, which again differ from poetical metres in the *other* direction, of being far more general and less various. These are concerned primarily only with the *first* division of the length of the bar,

which must either be into *two* parts or into *three*, giving respectively two and three main beats for a bar: this division into *double* and *triple* time is generic. The next stage consists in dividing the halves in the one case, the thirds in the other, into two parts or into three parts; and this creates species for each genus, the original halves still constituting double time, even where subdivided into thirds, and the original thirds still constituting triple time, even when subdivided into halves."[1]

These words bring before us certain essential facts concerning the nature of musical rhythm for which the emotional hypothesis offers no adequate explanation. It will be recalled that the two qualities of rhythm, which in the last chapter we maintained were of special emotional significance, are the beat or accent, and the tempo. So far as this reflex influence of rhythm upon the feeling tone of consciousness is concerned, it is sufficient if we merely take cognizance of the measures marked by the primary accent into which music is divided, and of the time-rate at which these succeed one another. But so we do not comprehend the whole subject of musical rhythm as it is known and used to-day; besides the accent and the tempo there is this exact mathematical analysis of time relation which to-day is one of the principal characteristics of rhythm as used by the best composers. The emotional theory of rhythm alone does not take account of this internal complexity of the measure, nor, if it did, could it offer a satisfactory explanation for this fundamental fact in the structure of modern rhythm. The emotional explanation, therefore, must be either supplemented or

[1] *Power of Sound*, p 137.

rejected. Especially is it incumbent upon a theory of music to-day when it is remembered that the tendency of modern music in its more artistic forms is away from the excessive use of accent and of exhilarating tempo, toward the more discriminating and intellectual use of this internal complexity of rhythm.

3. The author considers himself most fortunate in being able to give here some of the results of a new method of investigating musical phenomena, originated and made use of by Professor H. C. Macdougall, head of the Department of Music at Wellesley College. His method applied to Rhythm is this: an examination of hundreds and even thousands of measures in the composition of various composers is made to determine the actual nature and complexity of the rhythm. By a comparative study of the earlier and later composers, data are gained in a perfectly scientific way for conclusions as to the actual course of development in the use of rhythm. The form under which the results of such study are tabulated is as follows:

RHYTHM

Number of measures examined ...(normal..... non-normal.....)
Divided beats examined ....(normal..... non-normal.....)
Beats duply divided ....
Beats duply subdivided . .....
Beats duply sub-subdivided.......
Beats duply sub-sub-subdivided ...
Beats triply divided..... ....
Beats triply subdivided. ....
Beats triply sub-subdivided. . . .
Beats triply sub-sub-subdivided ..
Unusual forms of divided beat....
Division of units greater than one beat (specify them).

Types of the normal and non-normal measures
may be schematized in the following way:

Normal:

Non-normal:

The double or triple division of the beat refers to
the fundamental division of time into multiples of two
or three: the subdivisions to the degree of complexity into which one of these primary parts of the measure is divided. For example, when the beat equals a
half note it may be "duply" divided into two quarter
notes ♩ ♩, or "duply" subdivided ♩ ♫ and so
on to various degrees of complexity. Or, starting
with the measure ♩ ♩ ♩, the process of division
may be likewise carried on through the same degree
as, for example, subdivided ♩ ♫ ♩ or sub-
subdivided ♩ ♩ ♬, etc.

The following is a brief summary of some of the
results of the investigation:

Composer	Measures Examined	Non-normal Measures	Beats Examined	Non-normal Beats
Haydn	3,050	12.5%	9,280	9. %
Mozart	14,129	14.6%	6,464	10.4%
Beethoven	1,650	10. %	11,600	8. %
Brahms	450	25 %	3,830	16. %
Tschaikowski	1,300	23 %	13,230	9.3%
Liszt	590	32. %	6,400	17.5%
Schubert	325	34 %	1,850	46.8%
Strauss	400	44. %	3,900	52.5%

Although these studies of the composers named are
doubtless not extended enough to make the percen-

tages exactly characteristic, they do suggest a decided tendency to depart from the simple measure and decided accent of primitive music. Taking the figures at their face value, the only conclusion possible is that there has been a well-defined progress toward an internal complexity of rhythm manifested both in the measure and in the beat. Such is the evident testimony of these studies.

4. In seeking for the explanation of this development of rhythm, some suggestions may be had by reference to subjects longer studied and better known. The principles of mental development are uniform, whether manifested in the expression of man's scientific interests or in the growth and development of some particular art. Hence the presumption is, a presumption justified by all that is known or is being discovered concerning the evolution of mind, that in this development of rhythm toward a more complex inner structure, the mind has followed its usual course of progress from its early, crude, emotional reactions to a more refined, reflective symbolism. That is, the mind here turns from crass emotionalism to the recognition and employment of elements that come only by analysis and refined discriminations and are, therefore, more truly and more profoundly intellectual in character. Stimuli, which before were received *en masse* and were significant in proportion to their exciting power, are now broken up by analysis and their symbolic meaning more and more regarded. Let us see how this principle of mental evolution applies in the case before us.

In the lower stages of human progress the primitive, undeveloped mind naturally centred its attention upon those stimuli having the strongest instinctive basis, which, in the case of music, would be the rhythmic elements, the accent and the tempo. The appreciation of the more intellectual elements having no direct or vital bearing upon the immediate welfare of the individual comes only with some unusual genius, or by that long process of mental discipline known generically as education. Just as among primitive and uneducated people bright, saturated colors outweigh color-harmony, and all finer qualitative distinctions are lost in the primary, quantitative considerations, so in music the instinctive elements of rhythm outweigh the more intellectual factors involved. The process of all mental development is from the natural, instinctive, self-regarding activities toward the acquired, intellectual, and more abstract interests of life. This is true in the case of music as in all other phases of mental experience.

In connection with this thought, the conclusion of modern biological and psychological investigation, that in these primitive forms of mental reaction the emotional element is the dominant one, is pertinent. This is the widely accepted philosophical doctrine of the primacy of the will. Before intellectual interests were sufficiently developed to bear effective incentive and guide to action, the appropriate motor responses were guaranteed by the mechanism of reflex movement and by the impellant force of impulse and emotion. Mental development is that process of supplanting these instinctive and impulsive tendencies to action by intelligent, rational control.

Consequently in the earliest forms of music, and even far down in the development of this art, the accent and the tempo remained the two powerful factors in music, and were valued chiefly because of their influence over the emotional consciousness. In this stage music was more passive than active, more dramatically impressive than discriminatingly analytic. The mind had not yet acquired either the desire or the skill to break up this experience, but accepted it at its more apparent value; that is, as an appeal to the emotions. Such is the nature of the reaction of the naive and unanalytic mind in all of its interpretation of stimuli.

Later, however, through the training and development of centuries of experience accumulated and transmitted, the mind gains in analytic power and intellectual interests assume more and more importance. This new spirit of mental inquiry is by no means confined to the class of so-called "scientific interests," but being a new attitude of the mind, extends to all phases of the mind's activities. Thus intellectual interests are aroused and become even dominant in the interpretation of both religious interests and artistic phenomena. The history of philosophy is a long and accurate verification of this truth. There comes a time, therefore, when man will no longer be content to accept rhythm at its face value, but will discover that it, too, is capable of being analyzed and of being considered as having certain intellectual relationships. This does not mean that all this is done consciously and "out loud," with purpose predetermined—this is the stage of philosophical reflection—but that the mind will be unconsciously actuated by intellectual, as well as by emotional interests in reacting to such a stimulus even as rhythm itself. To advance to the plane where the mental attitude is thus changed from a reflex emotionalism to an analytic intellectualism, to state the development in extreme terms, implies a corresponding change in the content of the art itself, a content not before appreciated or even expressed. Mental development, let us repeat it again, means development all along the line, in creative power and in expression as well as in receptivity and appreciation. The conclusion, therefore, is that rhythm is no longer a purely emotional element, but as used to-day contains more intellectual attributes than when it served merely as an instinctive and reflex excitant for the emotional consciousness.

That each individual goes through approximately these same stages of growth and interpretation is a corollary following from the ontogenetic conception of evolution.

The method by which the musician utilizes rhythm as an intellectual element in his art is technical knowledge relating to music and need not be entered into in this connection It is sufficient to note merely that by thus making use of rhythm the composer has a new asset, a new method of expressing delicate relationships, balanced proportions, subtle symmetry, more refined antithesis, more effective modulations, a means of giving new forms to phrase and theme, of introducing greater variety in the development of a subject, and of emphasizing the unity of the whole.

Briefly stated, our discussion of rhythm has shown that it has been subject to the normal laws of mental development, and has passed from the stage characterized by crude reflex reactions of a pronounced emotional character to the recognition and realization of broader æsthetic principles as the true basis of its artistic value. The progress has been along the lines indicated above, (1) toward greater refinement in the expression of the emotions, and (2) toward a more intellectual interpretation of the elements of rhythm. It has been suggested also that music has now become so truly a mental construct with demands for logical development and order and well-proportioned unity, that it rests no longer upon mere tonal and rhythmical factors, but upon principles valid for art in any form.

CHAPTER V

MELODY

1. A psychological analysis of melody is an under-taking of peculiar difficulty; most of the obscurities and subtleties with which music is beset—and they are not few nor insignificant—refer to the melodic aspect of this art. Rhythm, because of its physi-ological and biological basis in the physical organism, and because it manifests itself in well-defined bodily reactions, seems to have a definiteness and concrete-ness not found in melody. Eminently adapted also to the psycho-physical method of research, it permits of accurate measurements and of experimental veri-fication. But when we turn to the subject of melody, no such direct or alluring avenues of approach are to be found. The physiological and biological relations of melody are neither so fundamental nor so sugges-tive. Consequently there is but little to be gained by following the method, which, in the case of rhythm, yielded such rich returns for the labor expended.

The reason for this striking difference is to be found in the inherent character of these two elements of music. Rhythm, as has been shown in the two pre-ceding chapters, is primarily physical, having an in-stinctive basis in the structure and normal function-ing of the nervous system; but melody, on the other hand, is as truly and as purely psychical as any of the most abstract forms of consciousness. True, it also makes use of the physical organism, but only as any other form of creative thought utilizes the body for its expression. If rhythm is inherently physical, melody, on the other hand, is essentially a true form of *thought*. So important is this fact for a philosophy of music that we pause, before beginning our analysis, to emphasize this truth by calling attention to two or three general attributes of melody.

2. In the first place music is fleeting, transitory, ephemeral. Though a composition is just as concrete, just as unitary as any other work of art, its unity is a unity *in time*, not in space. Consequently its attributes are not spatial, but like all attributes of consciousness, temporal. It was this fleeting character of music that moved Browning in his *Abt Vogler* to look for a transcendental basis for its perdurance. Be the value of his solution what it may, it does not do away with its empirical transitoriness, nor lessen the inevitable abstractness of a discussion of this element of music. As a phenomenon in time, music stands related naturally to literature, the art of conceptual thought. When judged, or even when appreciated, melody cannot be apprehended as a form immediately present to sense, but must be both judged and enjoyed as a memory. Only constantly changing sounds are immediately present to the ear; melody is a unity never completed except in the past. In this respect, as has been implied, it shows its essential character as a form of thought.

Another point often noted in discussions of the content of music, but mentioned here to justify further our conclusions, is the fact that melody is not imitative. In studying critically a painting or a statue it is regarded as objective, i. e., representative of some object or scene of the external world. Such works of art are meant to represent more or less accurately forms either actually existent, as in the case of a portrait or a statue, or forms that *might* be real objects in the world of existent things. Though not actual copies of external forms, they are, and must be, true to the *principles* of the external world they are meant to represent. This is not crass realism in art; it only asserts that if the artist does not paint objects as actually seen he must nevertheless still be true to life in its possibilities, if not in its actuality. Consequently the artist is guided in all his creative work by well-defined, anatomical principles of the external world. He is surrounded on every hand by models which, if not copied literally, are the foundation of his idealizations.

With music, however, the case is different: *the composer, even in the most liberal interpretation of language, does not look outside of himself for the models of his melodies, nor even for the principles according to which his works of art must conform.* The melodies in nature are, when musically considered, wholly insignificant. Think for a moment how meagre music would be, how vapid, if the law of imitation were as binding in music as in painting and in sculpture. The bird-calls in the *Pastoral Symphony*, for example, are introduced more as a novelty than as essential parts in the thematic material of that composition. The great themes of the movement in which they occur, as well as of all the others, are purely mental products only incidentally connected with the few notes forming the call of the birds they are meant to represent. And even in the most realistic examples of "program music," but little more can be said in favor of the theory of imitation as the source of melody in music. The use Beethoven makes of nature elements in the case just mentioned is typical; they are introduced now and then incidentally, but by no possible interpretation of language can they be said to serve as the basis of music, as objective forms are the basis of painting and of sculpture.

But if music is not the outgrowth of the imitative instinct, we are forced to the conclusion that as a factor in music melody is peculiarly and characteristically a product of the mind's own inner activity. Aristotle contended that music was the most "imitative" of the arts, but by "imitation" he meant a representation, not of something external, but of the mind's own inner processes. And in this sense of the term his statement is a very accurate expression of an important truth. It is probably true that no other art can express so directly or so accurately the real dynamics of the emotional life. But the point we wish to emphasize here is the purely mental or spiritual character of melody as an element of music. Music, so far as it is melodic, has no prototype in nature; it is not an element of the external world, refined and idealized or set in new relations, as objective elements are treated in the imitative arts, but it is *ab initio ad perfectionem* the result of the mind's own creative power. Some one relates that the whole theme for one of his famous scherzo movements flashed in Beethoven's mind as he stepped out one evening under the cloudless and starlit sky. Whether the incident be true or not, the principle is fundamental in the creation of musical works of art. They are created spontaneously in a sense in which no other works of art are spontaneous. That is to say, melody

is more independent of the external world, more dependent upon the activity of the creative imagination, than the elements of any other art. There is
philosophic as well as poetic truth in the well-known
words of Browning, which apply to melody as well as
to the harmony of the musical triad:

" But here is the finger of God, a flash of the will that can,
        Existent behind all laws, that made them and lo,
            they are!
    And I know not if, save in this, such gift be allowed to
            man,
        That out of three sounds he frame, not a fourth
            sound, but a star "

Beethoven wrote concerning his *Mass in D:* "From
the heart it has come and to the heart it shall pene-
trate."   These expressions are but various methods of
stating what must be regarded as the fundamental
psychological truth concerning the inherent character of melody: it is not a copy of anything in the objective world nor an idealization thereof, but an independent expression of inherent qualities of the
mind itself.

The conclusion that music in its melodic elements
is peculiarly psychical necessitates a certain method
of investigation and determines the principles according to which it must be judged and the grounds
of its philosophical significance ascertained. Since
music is not of the objective world in its origin, but
born of the mind itself, the true principles of its being
and criteria of its value are not to be found in any
principles of the objective world, but in the laws and
principles of the inner world of consciousness.   The
thesis thus stated is profound in its bearing upon our
problem; it means (1) that the broader philosophical

relationship of music can be appreciated only in the light of mental laws and principles; and (2) that the principles of a systematic, intelligent, authoritative, musical criticism rest upon the truth to be discovered by this psychological analysis. However, in our enthusiasm for the more fundamental subjective truth, the objective characteristic of melody must not be overlooked. Though subjective in its origin in a unique way, melody itself is an objective form and, as such, exemplifies certain important laws and principles due to its own inherent, architectonic attributes. These, in our analysis, must be given their proper consideration.

3. The two elements which an analysis of melody objectively regarded show are (1) the rhythm, and (2) variations in pitch. Rhythm furnishes, as it were, a background of uniformity upon which the various sounds in the melodic sequence stand out in more effective contrast. It is not altogether fanciful to say that thus is realized that ancient but not antiquated æsthetic formula, "unity in variety." The subject of rhythm in its principal features has already been discussed; we shall not therefore devote further time to this subject, except to say that it is in the melodic aspect of music that rhythm finds its highest opportunity for artistic development.

4. So far as variation in pitch is concerned, melody depends upon our modern diatonic scale, or, to include all possible modifications, upon the twelve tones of the chromatic scale. These scales having been fixed by custom and use, the sequence of tones in a melody is limited on the one hand by the interval of a semitone, and on the other, theoretically, only by the register of the voice or instrument; but even

in the case of an interval greater than an octave, the
tone must be one of the tones of the chromatic scale,
though in a higher or a lower octave. Practically,
therefore, it is correct to say that each melodic step
must be limited to one of these twelve tones. In
fact the variations are usually not so wide, for the
diatonic, not the chromatic scale is the ordinary basis
for simple melody. Stated in its simplest terms,
therefore, melody may be defined objectively as a
series of single tones rising and falling by definite intervals upon a rhythmic background marked by a
certain stress or accent laid upon tones at regular
time intervals.

This simple formula, however, by no means expresses the whole truth or gives us any insight into
the general psychological character of melody.
Though the successive intervals are limited to the
seven tones of the diatonic scale, to use the simplest
form, it is by no means a matter of chance or indifference what the order of succession of the various tones
shall be. Certain series of tones charm us and manifest all the power and unique beauty of a true work
of art; others, apparently not very different, are in-
sipid, meaningless or even positively displeasing. In
the one, shines the indescribable and undefinable fire
of genius; in the other, we feel the labored pains of
mediocrity trying ineffectually to rise. Can the difference from the purely objective point of view be
explained?

Continuing our analysis we are soon met with the
fact that certain intervals seem natural and easy,
while others are difficult to make. This may have its
ground in the relationships which come most obviously before us in consonance and dissonance

However that may be, the fact remains. For example, the octave, the third and the fifth are intervals for the modern ear readily made. But it soon becomes evident that the secret of melody does not lie in such relationships as these. The value of two successive tones as used in a melody cannot be determined beforehand by their relationship in the scale. The æsthetic value of two successive tones, as of two successive words in a sentence, is determined and determined mostly by the part they play in the organic structure considered in its entirety. This is an æsthetic principle of universal application.

5. Another principle far more important for a correct understanding of melody is the principle of tonality, the relating consciously or unconsciously of every tone in the melody to the fundamental tone of the scale in which the melody is written. As was shown above in the chapter on Musical Form, the fundamental tone of the scale is psychologically the point of rest and reference for all the various melodic changes in that particular key. In transposing a melody from one key to another, the inner relation of tone to tone remains unchanged, only the tonic or starting-point is raised or lowered, as the case may be. The psychological importance of this key-note is well emphasized by the fact that most melodies after gravitating back and forth to various distances from this point find their conclusions, their centres of gravity upon this note at the conclusion of the rhythmic period. As one writer tersely expresses it, "We may then understand a melody as ever tending with various degrees of urgency of strain to its centre of gravity, the tonic."[1] Or as Gurney with greater fulness

[1] Puffer, *Psychology of Beauty*, p. 182.

of words expresses the same idea, "The melody, then, may begin by pressing its way through a sweetly yielding resistance to a gradually foreseen climax; whence again fresh expectation is bred, perhaps for another excursion, as it were, round the same centre but with a bolder and freer sweep, perhaps for a fresh differentiation whereof in turn the tendency is surmised and followed, to a point where again the motive is suspended on another temporary goal, till after a certain number of such involutions and evolutions, and of delicately poised leanings and reluctances and yieldings, the forces so accurately measured just suffice to bring it home, and the sense of potential and coming integration which has underlain all our provisional adjustments of expectation is triumphantly justified."[1]

This description of melody, though unfortunately expressed, is, nevertheless, a remarkably accurate statement of just what occurs, as a melody is carried on from measure to measure, from phrase to phrase, to the final cadence. Who has not, when listening to some melody, run along a few notes ahead of the music to anticipate the coming changes, and has not found here and there a shorter by-path home than the composer has seen fit to follow?

The final word in a musical analysis of a melody is found in outline in the chapter above on Musical Form. A melody is a two-part or a three-part musical form composed of phrases and sentences with their rhythmic outlines and cadences. The musical analysis of a given melody consists of separating out these constituent elements in order that their individual character and mutual relationships may be more

[1] *Power of Sound*, p. 165.

readily and intelligently understood. But even so the secret of the value or the weakness of a melody has not been fully discovered. Of the principles of rhythm, of cadence, of phrase, of sentence, etc., a poor melody may be as true an exemplar as one of the best.

The truth is that such an analysis of form as this does not go deep enough to discover the real source of the artistic value or weakness of a composition. Form is important in any art, but form is not all; nor does it strike closest to the root of the problem of a psychology of art. Our definition of melody stating the character of melody in terms of rhythm and of variation in pitch was defective just at this point; while it was true enough of melody considered merely as a sound phenomenon, melody is that and something more. A better definition, therefore, would be, that *melody consists of a series of single musical tones in rhythmic succession expressing a complete musical thought.* This means that melody must be regarded as a form of thought as well as a sound phenomenon; and any theory that fails to state the principles and attributes of melody thus considered will be one-sided and inadequate. Having failed then on the basis of an objective analysis alone to discover the secret of the beauty and artistic value of melody, we turn to the subjective aspect of our subject to see if our quest there may be more successful. In other words, the discussion here turns to an examination of the suggestion already made, that melody, being peculiarly spiritual in character, that is, a product of the mind's own creative activity, must be evaluated according to psychological principles.

The method of our further inquiry, and to a certain

extent the answer to the inquiry, are suggested by the conclusions arrived at thus far. If melody, as has been said, is, in a unique way, the product of the creative imagination and not of imitative activity, then the true criteria of its value and the principles underlying its true character are mental principles, subjective rather than objective laws. Not only so, but the principles of the mind's activity for any particular type of mental reaction being uniform, the same standards of value that we apply to test the æsthetic value of other *ideas* will apply to music as well. So far as music is considered as a form of mental experience, therefore, we need not set about to discover some new norms of melodic value, but can proceed at once to apply the standards used as criteria of the value of other art conceptions.

And further, it is also evident that thus considered we should find the closest analogy between melody and literature, the most intellectual of the arts. This we shall assume without further argument to be the case, and shall justify the assumption only by showing that the criteria of literary excellence can be used also as the criteria of the value of musical thought. We shall begin with Unity.

6. In literature there is the unity of a single sentence, a wider unity in paragraphs, and likewise more and more comprehensively in topics, in chapters, in monographs, in treatises. In such forms the unity is a logical relation, and as it grows more and more inclusive it becomes commensurately more complex, more abstract. In the sentence the unity of thought involved is a single judgment; in the paragraph it is due to the dominance of a single subordinate topic there discussed. In a monograph or in a

treatise there is room for the wider elaboration of
material. This principle is valid throughout: as the
breadth of the subject increases the unity becomes
more and more abstractly logical and harder to appreciate. The unity in a musical composition is closely
analogous to this: there is the unity of a single phrase,
of the period or sentence, of a movement or of a
whole composition of the most elaborate type. This
is, in truth, but the subjective aspect of the structural forms outlined in Chapter II. Attention may
be called to one example to illustrate, and since for
illustration the simplest and best known examples
are the best, we give the well-known *Annie Laurie.*

At the end of the first phrase where the melody
rises from C, the tonic, to D, the mind is left unsatis-
fied, expectant. The tonic has not yet been found

at the end of the phrase. As the two factors pitch and rhythm both enter as constitutent elements in melody, it is only when the key-note or tonic comes at the end of a phrase or period that the mind finds its demands for unity fully met. Thus the second phrase balances the first and the tonic coinciding with the end of the period, the simplest form of unity is attained. The sentence is complete. But there follows another idea, technically another *period*, related to the first by likeness of rhythm and identity of key, which the mind readily accepts with the first as parts of a larger whole, a *composition*. Henderson, I believe it was, has said that the sense of incompleteness in an unfinished musical phrase is just as real, just as significant as the incompleteness in an unfinished sentence. The reason is not difficult to see; when we think a musical thought we think it in terms of rhythm and in terms of the scale in which the tonic is the ruling tone. To stop before the rhythmic period is complete or without a cadence, therefore, is to do violence to the fundamental laws of musical thought as much as to leave in language some phrase or clause unfinished.

What is true of simple melodies is no less true of the architectonic of more complex musical forms; although, as might be inferred, the unity of the latter is not so simple nor so readily seen. The unity of phrase and period in simple melodies is given almost as a direct impression of sense, but the unity of these elements in the movement of a symphony, for example, is so obscured by variations and exceptions that a more analytic mental attitude is required to apprehend it; in such forms the unity becomes as in a drama or in a novel, a mere logical bond, not visible except in the comprehensive envisagement of the work as a whole. As the scope of the work increases the unity necessarily becomes less concrete, more dependent upon abstract logical relations. Instead of a mere objective unity sensuously perceived, it is now a unity of organization. Thus the unity which the writer produces by the analysis and amplification and illustration of his principal thought and of subordinate topics, the composer gains by the development of his theme or subject. To apprehend such unity in either case is work demanding a thorough mastery of both the principal and subordinate elements, and of their logical relationship to each other.

But there is another form of unity in literature that also finds its analogue in music, a unity not produced by the development of plot or theme, but by what may be called *emotional congruity*. While this emotional unity is a factor in all poetry, in tragedy and in comedy, it is best exemplified in the lyric. How utterly incongruous, how impossible to judge the unity of Milton's *Lycidas* by the same standards applied to Burke's *Speech on Conciliation!* There is no logical development in the one case as in the other. The latter is meant to convince the reason, the former to control for a time the mood of the reader. But how congruous, how consistent, how perfectly in keeping with this *spirit* of the poem are the figures, the allusions, the imagery suggested!

Emotional unity in music is closely akin to what we have called the emotional unity of the lyric. There is the same dominance of one feeling state and the subordination of the content of the composition to this controlling mood. Not only are all shorter musical compositions like the song, the nocturne, etc.,

lyrical in spirit, but even many of the movements in
sonatas and symphonies show plainly the presence of
a ruling mood. Indeed, so far as the various movements are designed to express some particular phase
of the emotional life—as they are all intended to do—
they are lyrical in character. The influence of an
Andante or a *Largo* in inducing a dominant mood is
certainly not less than any lyric that might be named.
In such cases, however, it is obtained, not by specific
imagery pictured through language, but by purely
musical factors. But to whatever causes due, it enters vitally into the feeling of unity which every work
of art must in some way produce.

Unity, however, notwithstanding its supreme importance, by no means explains the whole æsthetic
effect of a work of art and cannot, therefore, be used
as the sole criterion of the value of any work of art.
There is, or may be, unity in insignificant melodies
as well as in melodies that are immortally great.
There is unity in things low as well as in things high
in the scale of life. Other criteria of value must be
applied therefore, before we get an adequate basis
for judgments as to the true nature and artistic value
of the melodic factor in music.

7. Literary criticism is usually divided into the
two heads, *Style* and *Content*. The principal elements
of style are *Strength* and *Gracefulness;* of content,
Originality and *Significance*. These four qualities,
we wish to show, apply as well to music as to literature, and may therefore be used as the criteria of
artistic value of melody as well as of poetry.

Strength in literary expression means that the
style is concise, direct; the thought is set forth in
plain terms without circumlocution or excess of figure.

In models of strength every word is an arch-stone; to take one away not only leaves a gap, but it weakens the whole superstructure. In such a style there is no surplus of verbiage, but the thought stands out clear and distinct, strong in its simplicity and untrammeled with ornament or needless detail.

The same principles apply in musical compositions: the facts just given are principles of style, true not merely in literature, but for any thought expressed in symbolic form. In music as in literature there is a thought to be expressed that the idea in one case is conceptual, in the other musical, does not alter this primary fact. Notes, it is needless to say, can be multiplied as well as words. And ornamentation is common to the two arts. A musical thought, therefore, can be expressed concisely or otherwise as well as a conceptual thought. Strength of expression, therefore, is a virtue of musical expression as well as of literature.

It may help to justify this conclusion and give a clearer conception of the nature of strength of style, to see what are the mental traits from which this quality of style arises. First, there must be clearness of thought, vividness of imagination. The strong writer must be fully master of his subject, able to see the goal from a distance and to know the most direct route to reach it. Strength of style, therefore, indicates a clear, logical, intellectual grasp of the subject in all its details. These details, however, will be neglected that the ruling thought may be clearly seen. Strength, therefore, is the attribute of the intellectual writer, whether he be poet or musician. Another mental requisite of the strong writer is richness of thought, profusion of ideas. Without this he will tend necessarily to over-elaboration and excessive ornamentation. On the other hand the strong writer, because he has such a profusion of ideas, will be interested to express the truth he sees rather than to spend his time polishing his style and ornamenting his diction. Browning and Tennyson with their strongly contrasted styles are an interesting illustration of the truth of this. Because of the very richness of his material the strong writer will not spend his time upon a worthless theme nor upon the inconsequential development of a good one.

The style of the Classicists, because of these mental attributes, is stronger than the style of the Romanticists. There is with the former a directness in the exposition of their themes, a richness of pure musical thought, a logical arrangement of their subject matter not found in the latter. There is less ornateness, less feeling, but clearer thought, more virility. Think, for example, of the simple motive upon which Beethoven's C Minor Symphony is founded! How direct, how simple, how powerful. "Such," he said, "is the knock of fate." And if the subject is laid down unmistakably, so also is the development not less logical and clear. It does not require the technical knowledge of a musician to feel the profusion of his ideas and the power of his thought. Though I do not remember the numbers of the program, this impression of force and confidence and wealth I recall very well, when the Kneisel Quartet years ago struck the first phrase of one of Beethoven's Quartets. So with Bach: there is this same thorough mastery of his thought and such a clear appreciation of logical development, that every note is justified by the rules of counterpoint. Brahms also

shows that intelligent mastery of his ideas which almost inevitably results in this direct and forcible
quality of style.

How different when we turn to the compositions
of the Romanticists, of whom Chopin may serve as
an example. In his music we feel not the strong as-
sertiveness of a mind thoroughly master of the situ-
ation, but more the musings of a strongly emotional
nature. Beethoven wrote because he knew, and
found joy in the expression of ideas so vividly real;
Chopin because he felt, and in his music found expression for the fire which burned deep within. In the
one case the man controlled his feeling, in the other
the feeling controlled the man. Beethoven made his
music obey the law of logical thought; his strong mind
would tolerate nothing else. Chopin gave himself up
to his musings, and his musical genius enabled him to
crystallize his mood in musical form. It is enough
to appreciate Chopin's music if one is susceptible to
the dramatic elements of the musical art. But much
of the beauty of Beethoven's music lies in its structural elements, in that elusive beauty of form which
demands for its recognition the keenest analysis and
the most attentive study.

8. Gracefulness, the second attribute of style, is
not so easy to define or to explain. Certain asser-
tions, however, may be made with confidence, notwithstanding the inherent vagueness of the quality
itself. Strength demands that a thought should be
expressed simply, concisely, logically; gracefulness
demands that it should be expressed in a pleasing
manner. In the first case, the thought is expressed for
its own sake; in the latter, elements of beauty must be
found even in the expression. The graceful writer

may be or he may not be as logical as the strong writer, but he must be sensitive to fine shades of feeling and appreciation of elements of sense beauty. His mind is alive to subtle distinctions, delicate shades of differences, so that anything incongruous or unharmonious is avoided instinctively. The thought of the graceful writer, therefore, is illumined with flashes of subtle wit, and his works are enriched with telling metaphor and simile. Suggestions are numerous, but his good taste leads him to select only those most proper and containing some element of beauty.

The same mental attitude applies to the composer as well as to the writer, and it will just as inevitably reflect itself in his style. The fundamental thing is that there be a mind responsive to such factors.

This virtue of style is, on the whole, not so rare as strength. The exact, logical mind is harder to find than the mind responsive to elements of grace and ease in expression. Strength is characteristic of a master mind; grace, a condition merely of sensitiveness. The examples of graceful composers, therefore, are numerous. Mendelssohn shows grace of a dainty, sprightly kind; not a little of the charm of Chopin's music is due to this virtue of expression. Grieg, notwithstanding peculiarities of rhythm, is graceful; Schubert, in a warmer vein, shows the same quality of style. But on the whole, Mozart, perhaps, is the best examplar of this style.

Of the two elements of style, gracefulness is the easier apprehended and consequently more generally appreciated. Grace in expression has to do more with the concrete, with the sensuous elements of music, than with abstract logical relations. The beauty of a graceful phrase may flash upon us, but the value of logical order, clearness of vision, can be found only by giving the closest attention, and consciously regarding the work as a whole. Thus, graceful music is more popular than music exemplifying strength. Though the thought be not so noble, though the content be not so profound nor so logically expressed, there is a sweetness, a finish, a simplicity in a graceful composition which all—the novice and the trained musician alike—appreciate and approve. And rightly so, for gracefulness is a truly æsthetic principle and merits our admiration. But I doubt if it can justly be given so high a place in the scale of æsthetic values as should be accorded the more intellectual element, strength.

When all is said, however, the real secret of a melody or of music in its broader harmonic aspect is not in its style, but in its content. If there is no really vital, significant truth to be expressed, even the most faultless style will hardly redeem the work from mediocrity. But on the other hand, we are ready to palliate a poor style, provided the content be of sufficient value.

9. The two principal virtues of a work of literary art considered content-wise, it has been stated, are Originality and Significance. Hadow, in his *Studies in Modern Music*, seeking for the criteria of good music, names vitality as the important factor. The composer, he says, must be the parent of his musical ideas, not their fabricator. The theme may come to his mind like a meteor flash, or grow more slowly into shape, but it must be given as it was actually seen, not as it has been described by another. There is no question but that he has here hit upon one of the

most fundamental requirements of a work of art. We would insist most urgently upon the legitimate birth of the musical thought in the composer's own imagination. There is no surer sign of mediocrity than to be servile to the models, even of the masters. The world little prizes copies of its masterpieces—they are sure to be inferior—but it is always ready to receive the interpretation of life of an independent mind. True, the recognition often seems slow in coming, but it is safe to say that little valuable truth lies buried in the past. The first thing for the creator of a true work of art is something worthy to express, some significant truth of life, some pictorial conception for the artist, some story representing a facette of life for the author, some theme or melody for the composer. There must be the splendor of a great thought else it will not be worth while; there must be the reflection of the man's own individuality else the subject will be trite; there must be the keen, true insight of the artist's vision else it will pall. When a man has such an inspiration as this, when his creative imagination pictures it in the medium of his art and his hand has expressed it in the symbols of his craft, lo, a new work of art is born. Does it satisfy the public taste or even the critical opinions of his time? It may, but it probably will not. Neither the public taste nor the critic's judgment is so profound that it must be taken for granted that they have fathomed the depths of art and understand all its possibilities. The true artist, the man of independent thought and keen vision, may be living before his time. His work may be prophetic and the world, including critics and savants, still blind to its truth. So it has always been, and so it will continue to be.

10. Significance as an æsthetic virtue is a protest against trivialities, a demand for things worth while. This attribute excludes the cheap and commonplace from art, and stands for dignity and nobility of thought. Things that are trivial soon pall, and the commonplace at best can please but for the moment. Art is serious and must be founded on truth that will perdure. Therefore only the deep things of life, the truth that changes not with fads and fancies, or even with systems of philosophy, the beauty that is beauty while mind is mind and man is man—only such themes can be the subject of great masterpieces in art.

An analysis of this attribute shows that it may be gained in two distinct ways. There is first what may be called intellectual significance; the subject may be treated in a critical, analytic, or constructive way, so that its logical import is better seen or its implications better substantiated. It is necessary also that subjects of this class should be intimately connected with the vital problems of life.

But a subject may be significant also emotionally; though possessing but little material for reflection, it has the power to stimulate to active consciousness some of the finer, but basic emotions of human nature. Such a work of art as well as that rich in thought must also be termed significant. To say that music and the other arts as well gain their significance chiefly through their emotional characteristics, is but to say that art is not didactic. Not only are the symbols of most of the arts too vague to give exactness in expression, a fundamental consideration in matters pertaining to the intellectual realm, but such an end is wholly beside the true purpose and function of art.

There is music, however, significant in both of these ways, intellectually and emotionally. The development of thematic material, the mathematical relations involved in rhythm and in harmony and counterpoint, the qualities of style productive of strength, are all intellectual rather than emotional in the mental reaction they produce. Bach's Fugues are the classical example of music of this kind. Not until their logical character is understood and their contrapuntal exactitude intelligently perceived can they be at all adequately appreciated. But not alone in Bach, but in all the classical composers, these intellectual elements are found as distinctive attributes of their thought and style, giving purity, nobility and depth to their music.

At the other extreme are the Romanticists and the modern school of musical "Impressionists," whose music is impressive through an appeal not to the intellect, but through its power to stimulate and to carry to a climax the human emotions. Since the emotional consciousness as well as the intellectual is a constitutent part of the mental life, its normal activity and its ideals are the basis of one of the mind's standards of value   Music may be significant, therefore, because of its emotional characteristics and power   The method by which music thus stimulates the mind to emotional reactions will be taken up for discussion in a later chapter.

In connection with this subject of the emotional significance of music, there is a distinction too important to be passed by without notice. It, too, is best seen in literature, but is valid also in music. In literature there is a scale of values of which Farce and Melodrama mark the lowest register, Comedy the middle, and Tragedy the highest. Tragedy marks the highest point of attainment in dramatic literature, because it leads us vicariously through the struggles of a human soul face to face with the eternal problems of fate, or destiny, or character, and arouses in us emotions recognized to be commensurate in importance with the problems involved.

An analogous distinction obtains also in music; there is a characteristic feeling-tone in the various *movements*, for example, as essentially a part of the psychology of the movement as is the dominant emotional element to these various forms of dramatic literature. On the one hand there is the light and graceful and sparkling *Scherzo*, joyful in its mood and care free in the mental imagery it evokes; but at the other extreme the *Andante*, the *Adagio*, and the *Largo* induce a mood closely akin to the deep emotions aroused by tragedy or by the sorrows of real life. Consequently the slow movements are felt intuitively to have more depth, greater significance than the more graceful, more animated movements with which they are contrasted. Life when faced squarely is serious—not therefore sombre—and only those things which get down to the roots of human nature and of human conduct are significant in the deepest and fullest meaning of that term. Thus there is abundant philosophical justification for the higher evaluation put upon that class of music to which Handel's *Largo* from "Xerxes," Tschaikowski's *Andante for Strings*, and Beethoven's *Marche Funèbre* of Opus 26 belong.

If what has been said in this chapter be true or even a fair approximation of the truth, it serves to call attention to a fundamental distinction between the inherent nature of rhythm and of melody. When we turn from rhythm to melody we turn from an element fundamentally organic and instinctive, to an element that is peculiarly psychical, a result of the free activity of the creative imagination acting spontaneously in accordance with well-known principles of consciousness. Instead of being like rhythm, connected with the activity of the whole nervous system in its functional activity, melody is, to say the most, connected only with the higher conscious centres. That is to say it is inherently psychical and its character and qualities must be stated in terms of the elements of consciousness. Thus we have in this chapter discovered what melody is essentially, and have stated what some of its subjective attributes are.

CHAPTER VI

HARMONY

1. For the purposes of the present discussion the subject to which we now turn offers some interesting features. In the first place the theory of harmony from the musician's point of view has been worked out in great detail and reduced to definite principles and rules. Discussions of this nature are therefore abundant. The fact that there can be rules for harmony suggests also that harmony, like rhythm, is a matter of exact and readily ascertained relationships.

Again, the subject has been studied thoroughly from the physical point of view by Helmholtz and others so that conclusions concerning the physical stimulus of musical tones have been scientifically ascertained and established. This does not mean that there are not many points still unsettled, but the fundamental facts concerning such subjects as the nature of sound waves, overtones, of wave combination and interference, the physical basis of consonance, dissonance and discord, have been established with all the certainty of scientific conclusions. No element of music upon the physical side certainly is better understood than the subject of harmony.

Historically considered, also, the subject of harmony is at a distinct advantage as compared with the two elements already discussed. In the case of both rhythm and melody historical data had to be supplemented by biological and anthropological inferences in order to fill out the account of their genesis and early development. So far back do they extend in the evolution of man that neither recorded facts nor tradition tells of their origin or of the time when they did not exist. Even in the case of the Greeks, to whom we turn instinctively almost for the beginnings of articulate philosophy and of art worthy the name, we find but little exact knowledge, and only the most meagre examples of music. The philosophers of Greece all agree in according it a high place in their civilization, but it is with music as with painting—we must depend more upon description than upon examples. But in the case of harmony all these deficiencies are fully met, so that all the value that comes from a genetic envisagement can be readily obtained. Harmony is an outgrowth from melody and in such recent years that we have recorded a very full, a very accurate account of how it arose, developed step by step, changed gradually the whole character of music and became finally the great opportunity and glory of this art, the one undisputed title of the modern world to independent art creation The opportunities for a genetic examination are thus too great to be entirely overlooked. We shall, however, only sketch the development in the briefest outline, limiting ourselves always to those facts which seem to have the most direct bearing upon the psychology of music.

2. In his chapter on *Incipient Harmony*, from which several quotations will be given, Parry says: "It is as if harmony—the higher intellectual factor in music —began with the first glimmerings of modern mental development, and grew more and more elaborate

and comprehensive, and more adapted to high degrees
of expression and design, simultaneously with the
growth of men's intellectual powers."[1]   The intellectual awakening of which he speaks is the Renaissance,
for the development of harmony as a vital factor in
music in its essentials is comprehended between the
eleventh and the seventeenth centuries.

Probably, as Parry says, it was due to the different
register of men's voices that the need was first felt
for having melody modified.   When singing together
it would obviously be inconvenient, if not at times
impossible, for both bass and tenor voices to sing
always the same note.   In such cases the first departure would be to sing an octave apart, though such
a distance would often be inconveniently wide.   The
problem then would be to find some other interval in
the scale which could be used with a pleasing, harmonious effect.   The two intervals after the octave
which best fulfilled these conditions were the fifth and
the fourth.   Parry's account of this stage of the development is so well stated that I quote: "It also
happens that the human mind is so slow to develop
any understanding of the effect of harmony, that men
only learned to endure even infinitesimally dissonant
chords by slow degrees.   The combination in which
there is the least element of discordance after the oc-

tave is the fifth, and after that the

fourth,   And these two were the first

which men learned to endure with equanimity.   It
took them centuries to settle down to the comfort-

[1] Parry, *Evolution of the Art of Music*, p. 84

able acceptance of such familiar combinations as thirds and sixths, and it took fully a thousand years after their sense of harmony had begun to dawn before they could accept the simplest discords without some preliminary devices to save the ear from being too roughly assailed by the sudden jar. It is a pregnant fact that the process has gone on till the present day, and that the combinations which human ears accept without preliminary and without protest have been largely added to in the present century. In later times the progress has been more and more rapid, but in early times it was most astonishingly slow. Men allowed some of our most familiar combinations as notes of passage—purely subordinate details—and by their use in that manner they became accustomed to the sound of them; but they were very long in coming to the state of musical intelligence which recognizes even a third as a stable and final combination. The test of complete satisfactoriness for any interval is the possibility of leaving off upon it without giving a sense of artistic incompleteness and a desire in the mind for something further. In modern times no chord is complete at the end of a composition which does not contain a third; but the mediæval musicians could not even put up with it in the final chord till the art had undergone some five centuries of development. Its relative roughness had much the same effect that a discord has to modern ears; and so whereas in modern times a man feels that he wants something more when he is without it, in mediæval times he would have wanted something more because he had got it."[1]

The first step toward harmony, then, was taken in

[1] Parry, *Evolution of the Art of Music*, p. 87.

order to meet the exigencies of fundamental vocal differences among individuals. At first this was introduced by having the same melody sung a fourth or a fifth above or below the "canto fermo" as the basic melody was called. This was merely doubling the melody at a harmonious interval, not harmony in the strict sense of the term.

The next step was taken when instead of singing the melody at a fixed interval they began to mix these three standard intervals, the octave, the fourth and fifth, as for example in the following:[1]

In the next few centuries musicians found out how to introduce ornamental notes, and so learned to like the interval of the third. Thus the process up to this point was essentially a long course in ear training, a process which we are told has continued even to the present time.

This, however, was not all of it. Another step

[1] Parry, *Evolution of the Art of Music*, p. 89

forward was taken when, instead of having the intervals determined altogether by the one fundamental melody, it was discovered that two simple melodies might be so combined that the result was not only positively pleasing, but something of an intellectual feat besides. This was the discovery that formed the starting-point which led primarily to the rich contrapuntal music of early modern times and later to the development of harmony itself. In the early years of its employment it is not strange to find that it ran to an illegitimate use, the intellectual interests and possible complexities proving a greater attraction than the simple pleasing beauty of harmonious chords. Metastasio, an Italian poet contemporary with Bach, and one of the most intelligent students of music of his times, says the previous generation was too full of figures and parts and contrivances to be understood or appreciated by any one except artists. They had followed out the new departure of combining separate melodies so far that its radicalism had destroyed its artistic value. However, it served a useful purpose, if indirectly, by increasing further the number of combinations musically allowable and cultivating an appreciation for the contrasted effect of such combinations.

To trace out in detail the various steps by which these departures from simple melody developed into the fugal architectonic of Bach and appreciation of chords for their own sake, would be to cover several centuries of diligent application, experimentation, and gradually growing appreciation of musical devices hitherto condemned. For centuries this was done in the interests of counterpoint, not of harmony, for the polyphonous effect produced by combining and blend-

ing two or more melodies. After a sufficient training of this kind the step to harmony was an easy and
a natural one. When these combinations of tones
were sought for their own sake and the old contrapuntal ideal was given up, then modern music was
born and only awaited the coming of the masters of
tone building to rise to its highest glory.

The psychological truth that evolves from this
survey, brief as it is, is (1) that dissonance is to the
natural unsophisticated ear displeasing, and (2) that
custom and training have a very large part in determining what combination of tones will be considered
as musically valid and right. Think, for example, of
the centuries it took for man to learn to endure the
third, and the part it plays in harmony to-day! But
of this more in another connection.

3. The various uses the composer to-day makes of
harmony can be classified as follows: first, harmony
for its simple tone or sound beauty; second, enrichment of melody in various ways; third, sound patterns expressed not by single tones in melodic succession, but by a series of chords; fourth, the contrasted
use of the major and the minor modes.[1]

4. The first use of harmony according to our
classification, the beauty of simple chords considered
as mere sound, is no small element in modern music.
This is the element which together with the structural elements of melody seem so all-important to the
Formalists. That there is some truth in their contention we would not deny. The sensuous element in
art is legitimate and important. Hence, instead of

[1] This last applies to melody as well as to harmony; but as this
seemed the better place to take it up for discussion, it was omitted
in the chapter on melody.

trying to belittle it, it is better to attempt to understand it. By striking on the piano a simple triad, as for example C E G, a new musical sound is produced different in quality and in character from any single tone or from any other combination of tones. It is readily explained from the physical standpoint why it is different; but just why it should be considered richer in character, is perhaps not so patent. The three component tones are such that the air waves producing them fall into simple commensurate ratios and the resulting wave has the regularity necessary for producing the smoothness and uniformity of a single tone. The principle can be graphically illustrated and is readily understood. In the illustration, let A B represent the wave of a given tone, and A C the wave representing the tone an octave below; when they are played together the waves combine thus losing their identity, the two giving instead a wave represented by the dotted line A D. In this

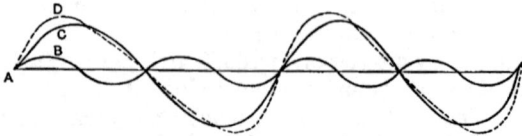

case we have a perfectly regular wave, but in more complex cases, as even in the simple triad mentioned, the regularity will be apparent only in periods of several wave lengths of the component parts. But why the resulting sound should be considered richer in quality and more pleasing to the ear, does not appear in such an explanation. The physical explanation alone, therefore, is inadequate.

The complementary explanation is a psychological

one, resting upon the principle that there is an æsthetic pleasure to be derived from a harmonious unity of disparate elements. This principle is as wide as experience itself and can be illustrated readily: if I am in a power-house and see an engine running smoothly, silently, I know the parts are all well adjusted to one another and are all working together well for the purpose for which they were designed. There is a pleasure in this apparent unity, even though I am ignorant of the purpose of it all. But if, on the other hand, I hear a throbbing or a jarring or the sound of parts in friction, I am conscious of a vague uneasiness at this evidence of mal-adjustment or lack of proper care. What is true in this particular case is true of all experience. Discord, consonance, harmony, are terms which apply to other than to musical phenomena, and in all cases they indicate this same unity or lack of it. While the feeling element may be particularly poignant in the case of musical sounds, it is nevertheless conditioned by a much wider field of experience. But whatever the explanation, the fact remains that certain tones when combined produce a richer, more pleasing effect than any single component tone of the chord, and musicians seeing this, have found that the principle is capable of great development and great power. Just as the painter finds in color as compared with black and white a richer medium of expression for old ideas and the possibilities of much new beauty, so the musician finds in harmony a richer symbolism for old musical thoughts, a means of increasing the sensuous beauty of his art and the possibility for the development and elaboration of ideas entirely new.

5. No small part of the epoch-making changes

wrought in music by the introduction of harmony are included under the second head of our classification, viz., enrichment of melody. Especially is this true in the earlier periods of its use; when the value of harmony as an element in music was recognized, it was first employed to enrich the common melodies of the times, hymns and secular songs as well. So highly was the innovation esteemed, so completely did it conquer the field, that to-day pure melodic music instead of being, as then, the rule, is now the rare exception.

To appreciate how preponderatingly harmonic is all modern music we need but to enumerate the various kinds of music and to consider the relative importance of the pure melody and of the harmonic elements. In vocal music, whether in opera or in song, there is almost without exception a harmonic accompaniment; music for choral singing is written in "parts"; orchestral music is so dominantly harmonic that the more common way to emphasize a theme is to give it added stress rather than to introduce it as a solo; and even the best solo instruments, such as the violin or the 'cello, are rarely used without accompaniment. But the fact is so evident that it needs no further confirmation; it will be worth while, however, to inquire a little more particularly into the artistic justification for the current practice.

In discussing the relation of harmony to melody Gurney distinguishes four stages: (1) where the melody is able to stand alone without harmonic support; (2) where the melody is not only enriched as a whole, but where the harmony is needed at particular points to bring out its point and character; (3) where the melody in certain places needs the harmony to prevent it from seeming incoherent or inane; and (4) where the chords have no definite relation to a distinct melody, but themselves present a definite sound pattern.[1] The last division corresponds to division three of our classification given above, and 2 and 3 are so closely related that there is hardly sufficient warrant for separate treatment. We may, therefore, give our remarks under the two heads: melody able to stand alone, and harmony used for the enrichment of simple melody.

As has been said, division (1) includes but a very small part of modern music. There are some melodies, however, generally those of Folk-song, which do not need the support of a harmonic accompaniment. These are the simple melodies of popular favor, such as *Annie Laurie, Old Kentucky Home, Kathleen Mavourneen*, and their like. The chief virtue of such music is in the simple melody itself; harmonization adds but little to their beauty and nothing to their popular favor. Their charm is in their simplicity, their palpable unity, their inevitable progressions, their perfect cadences, and partly doubtless to the universal and elemental emotions to which they appeal. But it is an open question at least just how far they should be considered true works of art. The other typical example is found when some melody or theme of more complex compositions stands unsupported for a few measures, but soon graduates into the richer sound of the harmony from which for the moment it had freed itself. In orchestral music this may be exemplified by brief passages in which the melody or theme is taken by some one instrument. But the age of pure melodic music is past, as evinced by the

[1] *Power of Sound*, p 250.

fact that such passages are used mostly for the sake of contrast.

Harmony finds one of its legitimate uses in an enrichment of melody, as a support running along in the same rhythmic sequence.   So intimately related are they, melody and support, that except for purposes of analysis there is hardly ground for distinguishing between them.   They blend in the listener's ear and are one in the composer's thought. As very familiar examples of music of this class mention may be made of compositions essentially melodic in character and yet the melody dependent for its point and character upon its harmonic support; such, for example, are the *Intermezzo* from the " Cavalleria Rusticana," Schubert's *Serenade*, Mendelssohn's *Spring Song*, and the like. The principality of these compositions is in the melody, for it is upon this that the mind fastens as the most distinctive feature. The ordinary listener will get the melody fixed in mind long before he has any idea of its harmonization.   Such compositions, because the principality lies in the melody, are eminently adapted for *Obligato* with solo instruments. And yet without the harmonic accompaniment the beauty of the composition is sadly lessened if not lost; the melody, important and beautiful though it be, is not able to stand alone, but requires the harmonic elements to reveal its beauty and to enrich it.

6. From music of this melodic character we can pass by slow gradations to music in which it is difficult to detach the melody from the whole harmonic *ensemble*.   Here, as in all developing forms, it is impossible to give an exact classification; the best that can be done is to call attention to typical examples

distinct enough to make the differences obvious.
Thus we have noted music in which the principal
charm is found in the simple melodic form itself; also
music in which the melody is still dominant, but the
effect is heightened and the beauty of the melody increased by its harmonic accompaniment.

In the next class the melodic factor is still present,
but it cannot be so readily detached, as it were. The
total musical effect is now more distinctly harmonic.
Such, for example, is Handel's *Largo* from " Xerxes."
The melody here does not stand out with quite the
distinctness that it did in the compositions named
above; and yet the melodic element is present and
still so potent that it is not incorrect to regard this
as the inner core of thought.

The last step in this progression leads us to the third
head of our classification—music in which the thought
element is not melodic, but in which sound patterns
are conceived and expressed by a series of chords.
In typical examples of this class of music it may
be impossible to dissociate any simple melody. The
chords must remain as they are or the whole value of
the music is changed or lost. The reason for this is
clear enough : a musical thought may be conceived in
terms of single tones in rhythmic succession; this is
simple melody, and the units of thoughts are the tones
of the diatonic scale. But a thought may be conceived also in terms of the richer units of chords of
varying qualities. In the latter case the music
would plainly be unanalyzable into melody and harmony. Thus Beethoven conceived in his imagination
the motive upon which the Fifth Symphony is based.

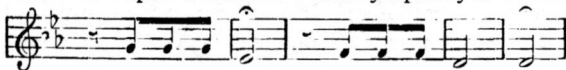

But he also conceived such harmonic passages as
this from the Seventh Symphony.

Or, as another example, listen to the following chords
at the beginning of the *Largo* from Dvorák's New
World Symphony.

And so we might instance other passages well
known in the musical world as, for example, the
Funeral March in Beethoven's Sonata, Opus 26;
and indeed no small proportion of the best music of
the great composers. In such music the component
parts are not single tones whose primary difference

is one of pitch, but chords whose differences are rather of *quality*. A definite musical thought may be thought in terms of pitch and the scale, or it may be thought in terms of related chords, differing in quality; that is, in key and mode.

Which is the higher form of genius, the power to compose a simple melody or a composition of this deeper harmonic character, it is needless to say. The minds that can create simple melodies and harmonize them are almost unlimited, but the minds that can conceive and express such harmonic ideas as we find, for example, in Beethoven's Sonata, Op. 26, are but few. There is a complexity, a subtlety, a richness in music of this character that makes it the ultimate test of the composer's genius. Just as the great colorists of all time are but few, so the masters of the richer vehicle of musical thought are not abundant.

7. Undoubtedly the most subtle effect of any of the harmonic factors in music is the psychological effect of the major and minor modes. For a long time the striking contrast in the effect of these two modes has been a standing puzzle for psychologists and physicists and musicians philosophically inclined; and it is a problem well worthy of investigation, for its solution would bring not only the satisfaction of an answer to this particular inquiry, but would throw much light upon the psychological problems now most puzzling to students of musical æsthetics. But before we start on our quest let us state the problem in its simplest terms.

If I strike the simple triad C E G, and follow it with the minor chord C E_2 G, the simple change in the chord, changing the E to E_2, produces a profound effect in the mental response to the sound stimulus. The psychological effect of the minor chord is generally, and I believe rightly, characterized as a feeling-tone of *sadness* or *yearning*. The same result is attained by playing the minor scale in which the position of the minor seconds is changed from the third and fourth, and seventh and eighth of the major scale, to the second and third, and fifth and sixth. These modifications in the scale and in the chord may represent for us the whole problem of the major and the minor modes, for these are the changes at the basis of the whole subject of these two modes. The composer, it is true, will find various ways to utilize the minor mode, but the psychological problem in all its essentials is found in these two simple changes.

As we pause to reflect upon the simplicity of the changes introduced, the thing that first impresses itself upon us is that such an apparently insignificant modification of the physical stimulus should be correlated with such a profound change in consciousness. To change the E to E♭ makes all the difference between the strong, confident mood of the major mode and a mood tinged through and through with sadness and yearning. Likewise the change in the scale, apparently a matter of indifference, would not and could not foreshadow the profound psychological effect which it produces. Such, stated in the simplest terms, are the facts in the case. The philosophical problem is to explain why such simple changes in the stimulus should result in the fundamental change produced in consciousness.

Professor Horatio Parker has suggested to me that there are probably many analogous cases in nature where a seemingly insignificant change in the cause results in differences of a monumental character in the effect. This is doubtless true. As examples of this in the physical world we may instance the different members of chemical series: of the oxides of carbon, for example, CO_2 is in itself harmless to animal life, CO a poison; the oxides of nitrogen also form a series, each with a powerful and characteristic effect of its own. Of the various oxides of iron but one is magnetic. HgCl is insoluble and non-poisonous, $HgCl_2$ is soluble and poisonous in the extreme. And so we might continue our list from the physical world, where the presence of an atom more or less in the molecule changes the salient properties of the substance.

But the most illuminating examples can be found not in the realm of the physical world, but in the mental. Here again the principle is true and of importance. For example, on the stage the step between tragedy and farce is notoriously a narrow one; change the accent but to the slightest degree, and tragedy is turned to melodrama or farce. In hysteria, the patient may alternate between periods of laughter and of weeping. The good will of a whole audience is gained or lost by a simple story or a mannerism. We often form our likes and dislikes upon some insignificant fact, and years are needed to eradicate the prejudice. But more significant than all of these is the way in which the emotions are aroused or stimulated; a word or an accent or a gesture may be the cue which unlocks the memory and floods the mind with emotions of a wholly different tone and color. Psychology has pointed out instances innumerable in which we see this principle active. Our associations are so made that with the emotions the law of a logical relation is neither the sole nor the most important one: the all-important thing here is to touch the proper cue, to waken the proper association, and the emotions come like a flood over consciousness. The case before us, therefore, is certainly not anomalous.

Helmholtz, as might be expected from the character of his investigations of the physical nature of sound, attributes the sad effect of minor chords to the dissonance introduced by the changed note. The effect of the E♭, to retain our former example, is not sufficient to destroy the effect of the chord, but it so veils it that it produces a feeling of mystery. In his own words, "The foreign element thus introduced is not sufficiently distinct to destroy the harmony, but it is enough to give a mysterious, obscure effect to the musical character and meaning of these chords, an effect for which the hearer is unable to account, because the weak combinational tones on which it depends are concealed by other louder tones and are audible only to a practiced ear."[1]   Gurney's objection to this explanation seems to me to be well taken. The effect of these foreign notes, he says, is to produce a slight element of dissonance. But why the dissonance, even though it typifies obscurity, should be interpreted as a feeling of sadness is not at all evident. If this were true, a dissonance wherever found should always be so interpreted. Such, however, is not the case.

Dissonance introduced into music in the major mode does not produce this characteristic mental reaction. This being true, it seems hardly reasonable to say that the melancholic effect of minor triads is due solely to the dissonance of the changed tone.

[1] Quoted from Gurney, *Power of Sound*, p. 271.

Helmholtz's explanation is valid so far as the physical stimulus is concerned, but it fails as a full explanation of the mental effect.

Gurney approaches the problem of the major and minor modes not through the minor triads, but through the minor scale. He introduces, therefore, some elements not recognized in the theory of Helmholtz. His own words will best present his thought: "If we ascend the scale of C and strike E natural, its nearness to F gives the motion a similar tendency to rise; hence the E seems able to supply the strength for the rise, to have got far enough from the D to be sure of its ground, to have its own balance and the power of making an independent spring which naturally gives an impression of *confidence*. If, on the other hand, we strike E flat, the sound keeps close to the D and seems dependent on it and willing to sink back to it; if we still advance to the F, we seem to press our way through the reluctant E flat, not to be sped onward as by the E natural; and this dependence and reluctance to advance give an impression of diffidence, a character which at any rate seems more naturally suggestive of pathos than uncertainty and obscurity were. Similar remarks apply to the F G A as compared to F G A flat in the second half of the scale: the A natural of the major scale is not quitted, it is true, by the step of a semitone, but it leads on securely and confidently to that step at the final stage; while the reluctance of the A flat to advance is even greater than that of the E flat, inasmuch as the instinct to use the B natural as the seventh degree in the scale, in view of the approaching key-note, is so strong that, if the A flat is used as the sixth degree, the motion has to make the long and

difficult step of a tone and a half. The same considerations, *mutatis mutandis*, apply to the descending
scale, the pathetic character in the minor descent
always attaching to the note which is only a semitone
from its lower neighbor not, of course, that the
pathos lies in the mere fact of the close proximity
(for at that rate C B and F E in the descending *major*
scale would be pathetic), but in the close proximity
occurring in the two cases where there is a *choice ;*
where the confident and independent A or E might
have been used instead of the diffident A flat and E
flat." [1]

This is the gist of his argument and the real basis
of his explanation. Although he admits that there
are difficulties in so doing, he holds that the minor
scales are the fundamental thing, and the minor triads derive their effect from the implied running of the
minor scale when the chord is sounded. In support
of this he says that with him at least the pathetic
effect is more poignant with the scale than with the
chord, and, second, that the minor triads of D and A
are very commonly used with the harmonies of C
major and yet do not there convey this pathetic impression. If the feeling of dissonance were the primary cause, this effect ought to be at hand wherever
the cause is found. Such, however, is not the case.

Whatever we may think of Gurney's own explanation, he has demonstrated certainly the inadequacy
of that of Helmholtz. The dissonance of the minor
chord, it is true, is the distinguishing characteristic of
this as compared with the major triad; but this dissonance, as Gurney has shown, may be present without the effect on consciousness ordinarily attributed

[1] *Power of Sound*, p. 273.

to the minor mode. Manifestly, therefore, there is
an element present which is not provided for in this
purely physical hypothesis.

The same objection will hold against the explanation which Gurney offers; to shift the cause of the
emotional effect to the scale does not fully meet the
difficulty. Consequently Gurney's explanation also
is but a partial one, as he himself indeed regarded it.
What must be done, it seems to me, is to turn from
the nature of the physical stimulus—never, however,
forgetting it—to the psychical side, to look there for
certain principles of mental interpretation. The
phenomenon we are investigating is psychical, and
its ultimate explanation can be found only as we
interpret the physical fact in the light of mental
principles.

Looked at from the psychological point of view,
the problem of the major and the minor modes becomes largely a question of how, in the course of
musical development, the characteristic emotions
have become associated with the two scales. To us
now the connection seems almost as natural and as
inevitable as pleasure and pain. Whether or not
there is such a nexus can be determined by reference
(1) to musical history, and (2) by a psychological examination of the relation between the stimulus and
the emotion, as shown in other and wider relations.

The modes in ancient Greek music were one of its
most noticeable characteristics, and as modern music
is a lineal descendant from the music of this people,
we look there for light upon the development of the
two modes of modern music. Parry's account is lucid and meets our needs.[1] The melodic scale of the

[1] Cf *Evolution of the Art of Music*, Ch. II.

Greeks, following the usual cadential inflection of the voice in speech, developed downward, not upward as is ordinarily thought to-day, and the first interval to be fixed was the fourth, counted in this direction. That is, beginning on our A, the fundamental interval would be to E with a third note a semitone above the E corresponding to our F. This was the tetrachord of Olympus. Then another note was inserted between the F and A which would give us the Doric tetrachord the nucleus of the Greek system of music. The next step was to extend this system by adding a similar combination of notes, with one semitone, the other whole tones. The Doric mode consisted of two tetrachords E F G A B C D E, with the semitones coming between the first and second and between the fifth and sixth. The Phrygian mode began one tone lower; that is. on D, and stood then D E F G A B C D with the semitones between the second and third and the sixth and seventh. The Lydian began still one tone lower; that is on C, and stood therefore as our major mode, with the semitones between the third and fourth and the seventh and eighth.

That the Greeks attached great importance to the emotional significance of these modes there can be no question. Both Plato and Aristotle in well-known passages leave no doubt upon this score.[1] But whether it was to the difference in the modes as such, that is, to the position of the semitones in the scale wholly, or partly to the pitch, it is difficult to say. We know that they attributed great significance to

[1] Plato, *Republic*, Book III, Aristotle, *Politics*, Book VIII.

pitch, abjuring both the high and the very low; but
doubtless, pitch was only one factor, for the Greeks
were far too sensitive to fine distinctions of sense to
overlook such fundamental differences as these. Besides, the difference of pitch between these modes
was too small to account for their clearly distinguished emotional effect. It is far more reasonable
to suppose that it was the mode, that is the different positions of the minor seconds, that formed the
ground for their distinction and for the emotional
effect attributed to them

It is both interesting and instructive to note the
emotional value ascribed to these three Greek modes,
for herein lies a striking contrast with modern
music. The Doric mode, with the minor seconds between the first and second and the fifth and sixth,
was the mode that taught manliness and self-reliance;
the Phrygian, with the minor seconds between the
second and third and sixth and seventh, the mode of
temperance and reason. Plato thus expresses the
value of these two modes. "I want to have one
(mode) warlike, which will sound the word or note
which a brave man utters in the hour of danger and
stern resolve, or when his cause is failing, and he is
going to wounds or death or is overtaken by some
evil, and at every such crisis meets fortune with calm-
ness and endurance; and another to be used by him
in times of peace and freedom of action, when there
is no pressure of necessity, and he is seeking to persuade God by prayer, or man by instruction and
advice."[1]

These two modes were the Doric and the Phry-

[1] Quoted from Monroe's *Source Book on Greek and Roman Education*, p. 160.

gian. The Lydian mode, which it will be observed
corresponds to our modern major scale, was considered *soft, voluptuous, orgiastic.*

In the light of such historical data as these it is
evident that the interpretation of the major and minor modes is not fixed physiologically or biologically
in the organism like physical pain and pleasure, but
is a matter of mental interpretation fixed by custom
and habit. Such facts, however, do tend to justify
Gurney's contention that the minor chords are secondary in importance to the scale; the striking emotional reaction to the latter antedated the existence
and use of the former by almost two thousand years.

But apparently the explanation of such interpretation of musical elements is just as far away as ever.
The Greeks interpreted one mode in one way, we
interpret it in another. The question, Why? however,
remains unanswered. There remains the psychological data relating to the subject, and to this we turn
for a final word.

Emotions of a full-hearted, joyous character are
physiologically excitatory, raising the general tone of
the system and producing stronger and more healthful reactions. The truth of this is matter both of
common belief and of scientific knowledge. We have
all been told that cheerfulness influences the diges-
tion, that hope is invigorating, and that good news
will reanimate a wearied body. Psychological ex-
periments, also, by examining the quickness and
strength of various muscular reactions and by testing
the sensitiveness of different parts of the body, confirm this impression of popular belief. On the other
hand, emotions of an opposite character, grief, melan-
cholia, sadness, etc., reflect themselves no less un-

mistakably in bodily reactions. These tend to produce a relaxation of the muscles, a general lowering of the tonicity of the system, and affect profoundly the activity of the various glands and organs of the body.

In brief, modern psychology is continually finding some new way to emphasize the fact that the bodily organism is extremely sensitive to all shades of emotion and is constantly expressing such aspects of consciousness through proper bodily movements. Attention is called to this relation in this connection to emphasize the fact that points apparently insignificant may be fraught with profound import when psychologically interpreted. Especially is this true in the psychology of the emotions, which in their rise and in their development do not, like the cognitive faculties, depend upon strictly logical relations.

Thus, what is apparently insignificant, through an inherited or a habitual connection, may flood the mind with the deepest and richest emotions. In itself it is a little thing that at times the voice is keyed up to a higher pitch, that the words come quickly and tend to group themselves both in thought and feeling in climacteric form; in itself it is not of any great importance that the voice is unsteady, faltering, subdued. At the most, objectively considered, these are but differences in pitch, ease of utterance and quality. In the one case the voice, we say, is firm and resonant, in the other faltering where it was firm, subdued where it was resonant and lower in pitch. It is only as these facts are interpreted subjectively that their real significance can be appreciated. Interpreted in this way, these qualities of the voice are just the qualities which, through ages

of development and fixation of meaning, have come
to be the most direct signs of the emotional life.

This firmness of tone is interpreted as evidence
of self-confidence, self-direction, a perfect mastery of
mind and body and of all the passions that human
nature is heir to; in the second case, some emotion
has disturbed this mental equipoise, and the mental
state is revealed in these bodily activities. Thus
qualities of sound, differences in accent, changes in
pitch, in intensity, in quality, in tempo, and even
changes from the customary order in musical progressions and chords, have come to signify or suggest
definite modification in consciousness. Back of these
sensuous differences, therefore, and yet implied in
them, are the mental conditions of which they are but
symbols. Looked at in this way—and how else
should symbols be regarded?—it is not hard to understand how even such apparently trivial changes
in the musical scales, as those which give the distinction between the major and the minor modes, should
have come to signify the most striking differences in
the emotional consciousness.

But the reader is probably objecting to himself
that, notwithstanding this circuitous approach, we
have not yet touched the real *crux* of the problem.
However, we have not intended to evade the issue,
but only to call to mind those principles which will justify us in our more specific treatment. We are ready
now to face the problem fairly, and to see if anything
has been gained. Coming back to our original statement of the question we ask again: Why is it that
changing the position of the two semitone intervals,
or striking the minor third in the chord, produces in
consciousness a feeling-tone of sadness or yearning?

The ordinary major diatonic scale is, both by custom and by education, the standard scale of modern music in the western world. That is to say, it serves objectively as the standard for intervals in melody; but more important, it is also subjectively the standard of mental reference, the form in which creative musical thought is involuntarily conceived. This thought cannot be too greatly emphasized. Just as we expect a sentence to contain subject, copula, and predicate, so we normally expect all musical progressions to be in terms of this scale. Whatever emotional significance this scale may possess, arises from the fact that it is a definite and fixed form of thought, the musical *alphabet*, if you please. When music conforms plainly to this recognized standard, there is a feeling of satisfaction and confidence, when it does not, a feeling of interruption of the normal process and uneasiness. Here as in other fields it is lack of conformity, *contrast to the rule*, that most excites the mind. *But in all cases, conformity to a standard is the secret of the emotional value of the major mode, unconformity the secret of the minor mode.* Thus, in the minor scale reading upward, the first two steps are identical with the first two steps of the major scale. This gives rise to an expectancy that the next step will also be a full tone, but instead it is only a semitone. The mind being disappointed in the anticipated result, hesitancy and uncertainty now enter where before there was certainty and the confidence of custom. The fact that the tone is lower, not higher than was expected, is also a delicate suggestion of what the resulting emotion will be. This disappointment is too strong to be healed by the natural order of the remaining notes of the scale.

In the descending minor scale, whether of the harmonic or the melodic form, there is the same interrupted sequence, and, more important still, the force of the tonic is thus destroyed; for as we descend the scale and approach the key-note, the mind runs ahead unconsciously as it were, and looks to the last few notes of the scale, to the satisfying tonic as a direct approach home. But here the order is changed, with the minor interval between the second and third, so that the force of the tonic when it is found is not recognized or felt. Thus the effect of the minor scale is to destroy effectually the normal order of the major scale, and to introduce suggestions at least, of sadness, by the tones being lower than in the standard major scale.

In the scale itself it is not merely the key-note, the tonic that brings satisfaction to consciousness, but the tonic in its proper, that is to say, its major relationship. Not merely the C, for example, but C found after the sequence C B A G F E D completes the scale. This is further evinced by the similarity in feeling produced by a minor scale, and a major scale descending, with the final key-note omitted. Gurney says that when in music we are longing for unutterable things, in reality we are only longing for the following notes. And so we are so far as the objective stimulus is concerned. So here in the minor scale, when we feel the unrest and yearning it produces, we are yearning in reality for the more natural order of the major mode. So far as the objective stimulus is concerned this is true, but at its best it is only a partial truth. The explanation is not complete, full rounded in its three dimensions, until we have come to understand how the differences in the sound stimulus have come to stand for vital considerations in the life history of the individual and of the race, and how through heredity and association they have become endowed with their present emotional correlate. This is just the point at which previous explanations have been defective. They have considered that the whole solution is to be found in the objective element alone.

But not so can any form of conscious phenomena be adequately understood or explained. We offer the above, therefore, not to supplant other physical explanations, but to supplement them. The major and the minor modes do differ objectively: this no one can deny. But these differences, instead of being the absolute ground of difference, are merely suggestions for the mind to apprehend and interpret. And the interpretation must come from the inner experience of the individual, either as it has been transmitted to him through heredity, or lived consciously and stored up through memory and association.

In conclusion, a brief summary is in order. Harmony, as our historical sketch of its development plainly showed, was not born like Athena, mature and full panoplied, but was a product of growth, and came to itself only through centuries of trial and experiment and of education of the mind to appreciate it. Beginning in the old polyphonic music as a variation of melody, in the course of some centuries of development it has come to be the distinguishing characteristic of modern music. To-day there is no music worthy the name of art that does not draw largely from this latest factor of music. And yet, while it has so vastly enriched music by providing a richer medium of sensuous presentation, by giving point and character and even new beauty to melody, by furnishing the composer with a new vehicle of musical thought and expression, and by making possible the current use of orchestration and of tone-color, it has not even in all this worked a psychological revolution in the inherent character of the musical experience.   It has increased the effectiveness of music and enriched the reaction to which music gives rise; but in the essentials music is music, whether in the simpler melodic or the richer, more complex har monic form.

CHAPTER VII

MUSICAL EXPRESSION

1. It requires but a moment's reflection to realize that without a chapter given to the subject of Musical Expression our psychological analysis would be incomplete Expression is, as it were, the acme of the musician's art, and through it alone is revealed the subtle beauty, the delicate antitheses, the grace and power of the composer's thought. Rhythm, melody and harmony are the three fundamental elements of music, but these without expression lose their charm and highest artistic worth. Expression gives to a composition individuality and life, redeems it from a mechanical sequence of sounds, and makes it reflect the most delicate nuances of the emotions, or throb with the deepest passion, expression is the life, the fire that fills the inert form with the pathos, the yearning, the sadness, the exultation, the hopes, the joys, the all but infinite longing of the human soul. The supreme test of the musician's genius is not in his technique, wonderful though it be, but in his power so to interpret a composition and to render it, that all its wealth of thought and feeling will be understood and appreciated by others acquainted with musical symbolism. Expression is, therefore, the final touch that reveals the hidden beauty of the composer's thought, and makes the elements of music reveal this beauty to the listener.

If expression is such an important factor in music, its analysis ought to give us some psychological truth of commensurate value. This may be either some new truth not discovered in our previous analysis, or some truth discovered before but here further emphasized. Since expression is the final touch of genius in the interpretation of music, an analysis of this subject should throw in the strongest light just these psychological principles for which our whole analysis has been made. We shall expect to find, therefore, in this chapter (1) further suggestions as to the motives and ends for which music really exists; and (2) added light as to the essential psychological character of music.

The first question to arise is, whether musical expression in its essentials is *sui generis*, or whether the principles involved are common to the other forms of art as well. The assumption upon which this book is written is, that in their psychological character, the æsthetic principles involved are common to all the arts. Thus far we have seen no reason to cast doubt upon this assumption, so we shall regard it as valid and proceed to apply it to the matter under present discussion. And further, since genetically the principles of expression had their origin in articulate speech, not in music, we shall turn from music to language to get the fundamental principles of artistic expression.

2. By expression in the use of language, as for example in reading, we mean the power of the reader so to interpret for us the words or symbols of the author's choosing that we may enter as fully as possible into both their thought and their feeling content. There are several remarks to be made upon this definition.

It implies, it wil' be noticed, that the words of the author may be meagrely or fully, clearly or obscurely, rightly or wrongly interpreted. So various are the meanings of most of our terms, so carelessly do we frequently use them that language, our most exact means of communicating thought, has been called a means of concealing, not of revealing our ideas. Allowing for the exaggeration, there is still a modicum of truth in the witticism, so formal does our use of language become that it is but seldom we ever have our attention directed to the exact or to the full connotation of any of our terms. Expression is the method by which some part of their original and legitimate content is emphasized and thus brought more clearly to mind. Language is symbolic, and in language, as in algebra, we use these symbols more mechanically than with a conscious realization of their import. Sully, in his *Human Mind*, in the discussion of the relation of Thought and Language, calls attention to "the tendency of words used repeatedly to drop their ideational suggestiveness and to serve in themselves as substitutes for ideas."

In written language, if the thought is not clear, we can turn back at will and examine again the vague passages until we have satisfied ourselves that we have gained the author's thought. With spoken language, however, the case is different. Here the constant and rapid flow of words limits the return to vague or to vital passages, while the rapid succession of symbols precludes the possibility of filling out the picture which the words only schematize. Hence, under these conditions, other means than the bare enunciation of sounds are invoked to make the communication of the thought more exact, and expres-

sion becomes a matter of the h ghest importance.
By means of the proper inflection and accentuation,
by changes in the rate of utterance and in force, by
means of tonal differentiation in phrase and clause,
the mind is so directed to the pivotal points of the sentences that the thought is made clearer, and the
appropriate emotional response is readily evoked.
Thus we see that from the very nature of language,
because it is an artificial system of symbols by means
of which thoughts are to be communicated, expression assumes a place of the deepest significance. The
same fact, though under different conditions, is true
also of music.

3. Further, our definition serves to call attention
to the twofold purpose of expression. As it was
there worded, the purpose of expression is (1) to communicate to the hearer as fully and as clearly as possible the intellectual import of the author's words,
the thought content, and (2) to impart the emotional state which accompanied, or enriched, or inspired his words. The truth of this is obvious in acting or reading or in oratory or, indeed, in all uses of
spoken language, whether the purpose be to convince
by logical reason, or to persuade or to excite or to
calm the hearer. The relative importance of the two
purposes will vary, however, and between wide extremes, with the character of the discourse.

The distinction just made is one that needs all
emphasis, for it touches the heart of the problem of
expression in art, and sheds a wonderful illumina-
tion upon the deeper problem of the true purpose
and function of art. Followed out carefully, I am
convinced that it would help to clear up many of
the obscurities that cluster around the philosophy

of the several arts, and would resolve many of the generalities with which discussions of this subject are often burdened.

The relative value of the emotional and the intellectual factors in expression, it has been said, depends primarily upon the character of the work of art to be thus interpreted. In the one case, the principal object will be to make the thought content clear and vivid, in the other, to make the listener feel the emotions that throbbed warm in the consciousness of him who was thus moved to express his thought in artistic form. There are some to whom Browning with his richness of thought, his philosophic attitude of mind, seems the true poet; others, the majority, perhaps, prefer Tennyson with his finished phrases; still others find in the burning thoughts of Shelley or the intense fervor of Keats the highest type of the poetic art. But whatever the extreme to which the poet may go, whether toward intellectualism or toward emotionalism, the intellectual element is never solely present, nor ever altogether absent. In literature there is always thought, always emotion, and to interpret and to communicate these two essential elements is the true function of expression.

The same twofold purpose of expression holds true of expression in music. The character of the thought to be expressed and the symbols used are different, but the double function of expression remains nevertheless. As has been shown above, the formal, architectonic side of music is an integral part of its reality, and as such is deserving of intelligent recognition and appreciation. To disregard all this in the enthusiasm for a more impressive and emotional apprehension of music is not only to neglect an important element, but it is to vitiate the pleasure and satisfaction which the composition was designed to give.

But to be enjoyed these intellectual elements must be appreciated at their true worth, and to be appreciated they must be understood, and to help to a more intelligent understanding of the architectonic of a composition is one of the distinct purposes of expression. Thus there is a place for expression in the rendering of even the most classical forms of music.

Our previous analysis has demonstrated also that there is in the musical experience a strong emotional element. To communicate this to the listener in its more delicate nuances as well as in its deeper and more intense climaxes, by the modification of the sound stimulus, is also part of the interpretation of the composition. To do this is the second purpose for which expression is demanded. Thus expression in music is just as vital, just as urgent as in speech; and furthermore it exists for exactly the same reasons. Some elucidation of the means of musical expression will serve to justify this conclusion.

4. The principal elements of expression utilized to make clear the logical structure of the composition are (1) variations in force, as in the clear enunciation of a melody or of some melodic factor or harmonic pattern, and (2) marking off distinctly by the proper accent the unitary measure and the rhythmic phrase.

Modification of force or intensity, as will be shown a little later, is a powerful means of giving emotional expressiveness to a composition, but it is also a means hardly less fundamental in making the structural elements of music readily discernible. Our present remarks are confined to this latter use. Though it may be utilized in several ways, the principle involved is a simple one. Increased force is the natural way of drawing attention to a particular structural element by making it sensuously more impressive. It is a fundamental law of attention that a strong stimulus gains the focus of consciousness and thus rises in clearness and vividness. Thus, when it is necessary that a structural element should be accentuated more than others, the simplest method of thus setting it apart is to lay added stress upon it. For example, in melodic compositions, where the principality lies in the melody, it is necessary that the mind should fasten upon the melody and differentiate between this and the harmonic accompaniment. So, also, in thematic music much can be done to help the listener to a more intelligent conception and appreciation by emphasizing the theme and its variations so that it and they can be more readily distinguished. In orchestral music, where the conductor has such varied timbre effects at his command, much can be done by utilizing these effects; but the need for accentuation through added stress is by no means obviated even here.

Another opportunity to make the logical relations of a composition clearer by this same device is found in thus pointing out harmonic phrases and patterns as well as melodic elements. In brief, wherever there is a structural element, phrase, motive, theme or melody which the mind should grasp clearly in its inner relationships and in its relation to the whole, one of the most obvious ways to gain this end is through a modification of the force with which such a part is played.

It is needless to add that modifications of force for

the sake of emphasis include the use of *piano* and *pianissimo* as well as *forte* and *fortissimo*. Through contrast, both in speech and in music, the former is just as impressive as the latter.[1]

The other way in which expression by modifications of force assists in the intellectual appreciation of a musical composition is found in connection with rhythm. A musical composition in its rhythm has a background of mathematical precision. If this is to mean anything more than an opportunity for the reflex response to accented beat of the measure, it must be made so by so marking out the larger rhythmic structure that it will be readily and consciously perceived Lussy, in his work on *Musical Expression*, classifies the principles of musical expression under three heads: (1) the *metrical accent*, which appeals to the instinct; (2) the *rhythmical accent*, appealing to the intellect; and (3) the *expressive accent*, making its appeal to the emotions. And he is right so far as he makes the accent of the measure instinctive, though it also appeals to the emotions, and in making the "rhythmical accent" of intellectual significance. The "metrical accent," also, as he calls it, is not altogether without intellectual significance, as has been amply

---

[1] The universal tendency of students, both in oral and in musical expression, is to overlook such distinctions and merge all into an undifferentiated body of sound. Witness the monotonous drawl or the sing-song style of the boy or girl learning to read, or the equally noticeable uniformity of those beginning the study of music. Playing without expression is altogether analogous both in cause and effect to the monotonous reading of the child; there is a failure in each case to grasp the thought relations, to see the force of any part, and consequently an utter absence of power to make those relations evident to others. A thorough understanding and appreciation of the composition, therefore, is the first step toward expression.

shown above. But the more important accent, from the intellectual point of view, *is* the *rhythmical*, as he calls it, the accentuation of the phrase and the larger rhythmic patterns. In the first part of the chapter upon this subject he thus expresses the purpose of rhythmical accentuation: "A performer must be able to distinguish the rhythmical phrases, so as to feel the initial and the final notes of each, and bring them into relief. Bad phrasing is like bad punctuation and bad accentuation in reading, and it is as important in music to phrase and to accentuate according to the natural tendency of the notes and the laws of attraction by which they are grouped and by which they gain their meaning, as it is to give to each word, sentence, or part of sentence, its due form."

That these relations are purely musical, not conceptual as in language, to the uninitiated, makes them seem more abstract, more intangible. But they exist, nevertheless, and are part of the very essence of music. To understand this structural organization of a composition, therefore, must remain one of the true ends of the musical experience, and for this reason, one of the purposes of musical expression. Art in its highest works is no formless, impressionistic affair, the whole purpose being to affect the emotions or to deceive the intellect, but it is true to the principles of the intellectual, as well as of the emotional life. Thus, it is evident, there is truth in the words quoted above, and rhythmical phrasing and rhythmical accentuation, made apparent through expression, are to music what punctuation and accentuation are to language—a means of giving a clearer intellectual comprehension of the logical or thought content of the composition.

5. But when the term "expression" as applied to music is used, it is to the emotional rather than to the intellectual aspect of the subject that popular thought refers. To play "with expression" is to render the composition so that the emotional consciousness is stimulated in the most effective way. There is a certain justification for thus giving precedence to the emotional element, though no excuse, certainly, for ignoring the intellectual element. The real function of art is not to instruct, not to develop intellectual acumen or breadth of view, but to give play to the emotions in the plane of the ideal and the beautiful. Hence even the intellectual elements in music exist for the sake of the æsthetic emotions they produce.

It is in the province of these emotional elements in music also where it is too commonly thought that principles and laws do not obtain. Art, it is said, is above all law, and the emotions, like the winds, come and go, but their causes are never seen. This view, however, is most certainly erroneous. It is true that the psychology of the emotions is still but imperfectly understood, but to contend that the emotional consciousness is without its own laws and principles is to contradict the postulates upon which all psychology is based. If this be true, there are principles of emotional as well as of intellectual expression.

As the most common and efficient means of thus increasing the emotional effect of music, we shall call attention to three devices at the command of the musician: (1) modifications of force, (2) modifications of tempo, and (3) peculiarities in the sound stimulus produced by what is known generically as "touch."

The simplicity of these three elements of expression is perhaps their most noteworthy characteristic. Although the emotional effects produced are subtle in the extreme, the means by which such effects are produced are of surprising simplicity. Herein lies the mystery of the emotional life.

The three factors given are by no means peculiar to music, but are strictly analogous to modifications of the voice in speech, whereby the speaker is enabled to stir up the emotions of his hearers, now arousing them, as did Antony, to the heights of passion, now calming them to the most serious contemplation of the issues of life and death. In this way he gains a power over his audience which his logic alone could never give. It is upon these same sense qualities, too, that the demagogue relies for his influence with the masses, and by factors of like nature that the mob spirit spreads like contagion. Though they are all when analyzed nothing more than sensuous qualities of sound, this does not lessen their effect or destroy their power.

One need not listen long to an effective speaker to find these three points many times illustrated. Now his words, if the discourse is descriptive, run evenly with the inflection directed more to a clear expression of the thought than to move his hearers to strong emotional reactions; but when occasion for the latter comes, all his energy is thrown in the utterance of a few words, or with masterly skill he so modifies his voice in speed and strength that his listeners follow involuntarily all the movements of his emotional consciousness. Through it all, the burst of sudden power, the continued monotone, the lowered voice in phrase or sentence, the mere intensity of the sound is the barometer that registers accurately his own emotional states.

Just as readily can the observer note constant variations in the *rate* of utterance if the speaker be at all susceptible to the finer possibilities of language. At one time, stimulated by some strong, exciting emotion, the words may fairly pour from his lips, at another, when thought is deadened by some depressing emotion, the machinery of speech works slowly; and this by the observer is properly interpreted as symbolic of his emotional life.

Corresponding to the last division of the elements of emotional expression, *touch*, the speaker has characteristic ways of enunciating his words, thus giving them a direct, impressive, emotional value. Now his voice may be firm and steady, resonant with strength, or tremulous, or deliberative. Such qualitative distinctions also have emotional significance.

If this be true, and the principles of emotional expression in music are found also in articulate speech, it follows that musical expression is not some mysterious, inexplicable quality of personality, but merely a particular application of laws as old and as universal as language itself. To possess the rare gift of making use of them is musical genius, but to understand their application is nothing more than a little psychological knowledge of one particular aspect of art.

The application of this truth to music, as has just been said, is easy, though to put it into practice is the severest test of the musician's genius and skill. Take first, modification of force. Plainly, as the condition for making proper artistic use of this element of expression, there must be deep, true feeling on the part of him who is interpreting the composition. But the power to feel deeply—not merely intensely—is one of the surest attributes of maturity, Nature's compensation for the joys of childhood forever lost, the best insurance against *ennui*, the supreme test of the artistic temperament. Technically it is called "musical feeling." In songs, in oratorio, in opera, where the words are a guide to the sentiment, expression is, or should be, to the thoughtful person comparatively easy. But in instrumental music, where there is no such infallible clue to the feeling content, its correct interpretation becomes a matter of far greater difficulty. Here, only unusual musical genius or the most finished education, or both, will enable one to compass the full emotional possibilities of a masterpiece. To give expression to this feeling much can be gained through appropriate modifications in force. So closely have differences in the quality and intensity of the voice become associated with emotional expression that even such differences in musical sound are instinctively thus interpreted.

From a natural, instinctive basis for emotional reactions to intensive differences in sound stimuli, the musician by a long process of training and education develops a refined susceptibility for such modifications until this becomes one of the most direct, most powerful excitants of the emotional consciousness.

Modifications in its time rate, also, being one of the attributes of the emotional consciousness which normally finds expression in bodily reaction, the various emotions have come to be symbolized in this physical expression. The stream of consciousness is one of the most variable streams in the world, and

one of its marked characteristics is its ever-changing
rate of flow; now it is hurrying on with all speed to
some emotional climax, now it moves leisurely with
no distinct end in view, and now laboriously, and all
but stops because of the obstacles that impede its
chosen path of progress. All these mental changes
are faithfully reflected in the organism. Now since
this ever-changing rate of movement is one of the
fundamental attributes of consciousness, those factors which signify it—and speech and musical sound
are included under this head—will have a strong
effect upon the mind. Thus the tempo with which a
composition is rendered will exert a strong impressive, suggestive emotional influence over consciousness. The unchanging rhythm of a popular waltz or
a quickstep of metronomic accuracy is monotonous,
and hence tends to deaden, not to stimulate, that
delicate play of the emotions essential to a genuine
artistic experience. The natural play of the emotional consciousness is not so uniform as this. Now
the current is slow, now fast, now leisurely, now aim-
less, now shallow, with ripples of laughter and joy,
now deep and quiet. All this can be typified in
musical sound, suggested in the tempo. To use this
factor artistically, so that the emotions will be ap-
pealed to naturally and strongly, is a part of good
expression.

By *touch* the musician understands the style of
striking the keys of a musical instrument so that different qualities of sound are produced. *Staccato* and
Legato are the two principal styles, though so far as
the effect is concerned, *Tremolo* and all such related
and contrasted effects should be included. Staccato
passages usually produce the light and airy effect of

a minuet, for example, while the legato is used to indicate depth and intensity of feeling.

By means of these comparatively simple modifications of musical sound, the musician is able to make music an art of wonderful beauty and power, and to play over the whole gamut of man's emotional consciousness with the directness and effectiveness for which music is justly esteemed remarkable. Just why musical symbolism exerts such power over consciousness will be inquired into in the next chapter.

In conclusion, we pause only to reaffirm what was premised in the beginning of the chapter. Musical expression rightly understood has a twofold purpose, viz., to illumine the intellectual element in music by enabling the listener to see the structural relationships more clearly, and to accentuate the emotional element, especially in its higher and more refined nuances. Thus the chapter further justifies the conclusion toward which the whole analysis has been leading, viz., *that music is both intellectual and emotional in its content, and that it is true to the principles of art in general.*

PART III

THE PHILOSOPHY OF MUSIC

CHAPTER VIII

THE UNIVERSALITY, THE VERSATILITY AND THE POWER OF MUSIC

1. Thus far music has been subjected to a psychological analysis in order to determine the character of its various elements and the nature of the psychological reaction to which these elements give rise. All of this is a necessary prolegomenon to the conclusions to be formulated in the remaining chapters. But with the chapter on Musical Expression this analysis is completed, and the trend of the discussion at this point becomes more strictly philosophical.

At the very beginning of the discussion attention was called to three general attributes that belong to music considered as a form of art, viz, its universality, its versatility, and its power. The subject is worth pursuing a little farther. Besides the interest inherent in the question of the causes for these attributes belonging to music in so marked a degree, the problem thus raised gives an excellent opportunity to test pragmatically the validity of the analysis we have just completed. Why, then, is music the most popular of the arts? Why does it have such versatility? And how shall we explain its power?

The principal reason for the universal appeal music in some form makes to mankind lies in the fact that rhythm, always an indispensable element in music, has an organic or instinctive basis. Among those who have ears to hear and minds trained to perceive the true beauty of music as an art, nothing more than its own inherent worth as a form of art is needed to give it favor But music is different from the other arts in having as its basis a factor which can be traced far beyond the limits of the proper realm of art. Man's nervous system is so constituted that it attunes itself automatically, as it were, to a rhythmic stimulus and with a pleasurable concomitant strong enough to insure a decided preference for such form of stimulation. The mental response to music with a pronounced rhythm is, therefore, for the most part merely a passive and reflex response to a stimulus which, in the course of time, has acquired a direct and a powerful influence over consciousness. Response to such music, therefore, is both easy and pleasurable, qualities which in any connection will win a large and a demonstrative, if not a very discriminating audience. Thus music even in its more primitive, pre-artistic forms is peculiarly fitted to win popular favor. The instinctive elements upon which other arts are based, with the possible exception of poetry, which like music is based upon rhythm, are not so fundamental in the organism, nor so strong in their appeal to the undeveloped mind.

In connection with this fact it should be remembered, as was brought out in the chapter on Rhythm, that the mental response given to rhythm even in these more primitive forms is emotional, and that emotional activity is normally the most attractive, the most seductive form of all mental activity. Volitional and intellectual activity, since they require attention, are both, as such, fatiguing, and are usually engaged in for the sake of some ulterior end; but emotional activity is an end in itself and so draws stronger upon primitive instincts than the two other forms of mental processes. The emotional factors in music, in the course of man's progress toward his present intellectual stature, have been discovered, utilized and appreciated, so that music, in the broader use of the term, can claim for its adherents now and in the past thousands who could have no conception of the nature of music as a true form of art. Thus there is a palpable ambiguity in the use of the term, and music as a true form of art probably benefits in its reputation by the vagueness in which the term is used.

But even in the narrower connotation of the term, music has an advantage over the other arts in the strength of the instincts upon which it rests. The instinctive reaction to rhythm, we have seen, is not lost even in the highest forms of music.

However, music is not all instinctive; in the highest forms of music in which thought elements and opportunities for refined emotional reactions are found, the charm is not in the rhythm, though conditioned by it, but in the æsthetic value of form and content intelligently apprehended. If music did not thus develop with the developing mind, it would have been outgrown and cast aside as worthless, except as an effective means of bodily and emotional stimulation. But music *has* developed and become a true art, and as such pleases thousands who have passed far beyond the love of stirring rhythm for its own sake. Thus, the instinctive nature of rhythm, the emotional reaction to which it gives rise, and the fact that as a true form of art it retains the force of these primitive

instincts, all combine to make music one of the most
universal forms of the arts.

One further point must be touched upon, though
it will be discussed more in detail in connection with
the power of music. I refer to the fact that music is
the art of *sound*, and sound, being the most common
and effective way of communicating both thought
and feeling, the race has been well trained in susceptibility to tonal distinctions.

2. By the versatility of music we mean the unique
power which this art possesses to stimulate in the
human mind, emotions of the most varied character
both in their mental coloring and in the bodily reactions to which they give rise. As was pointed out
in the first chapter, music can arouse enthusiasm,
stifle bodily fatigue, instill courage and endurance,
animate the mind with gayety, or calm it when excited to religious meditation and worship.   Whether
the emotion be of joy or grief, of excitement or repose, of comedy or tragedy, music can deepen the
note of sadness or heighten the touch of joy, add
fervor to religious worship, or excite to deeds of reck-
lessness. For a discussion of the deeper phases of
music this fact calls for some explanation. A comparison of music with the other arts in this respect
will serve to suggest the truth we seek.

The emotions that architecture and architectural
elements engender are relatively pure and of a very
decided intellectual character. As the relationships
are all structural and formal, the appeal is primarily
to the intellect and the emotions are thus aroused.
There is little or no appeal to instincts connected
intimately with the direct well-being of the individual or with the more dynamic emotions.   Painting

and sculpture also, while they can picture scenes of
tragic import, or the heroic, or even scenes of hu-
morous nature, confine their influence largely to
the more formal æsthetic emotions, which in character are contemplative and therefore largely passive. The purely sensuous factor even of color
does not play such a very important part as an
emotional excitant. There are but few of the human race whom color excites as it does the tradi-
tional bull.

Music has all the purely formal beauty of these
arts, stimulating the mind as do they to the intellectual æsthetic emotions; but it gives rise besides to
emotions that are powerfully exciting and directly
and dramatically impressive. In its emotional significance, therefore, music stands in striking contrast to these arts.

Literature is the one art besides music that has the
power to any large degree to engender these more
dynamic emotions as well as to charm by the more
quiet and contemplative æsthetic sentiments. Besides the pure impartial feelings due to the artistic
beauty of a masterpiece of literature, a work of art
in this field may fire the heart with zeal, excite it
to brave deeds or self-denial, awaken the strongest
feeling of sympathy and partisanship, fill the heart
with longing, or bring the reflective attitude of religious worship and prayer. Literature and music
therefore must be classed together in their power to
play widely upon the emotional consciousness, and to
engender other emotions than the purely æsthetic
ones arising from elements of formal beauty there
expressed. They both have the power to control the
emotional consciousness in its broader and more dy-

namic aspects as well as in the restricted realm of pure art feeling.

But notwithstanding the close similarity in the emotional results obtained in the two cases, the means by which this effect is produced stand in striking contrast. Literature, being the art of articulate speech, is definite and exact in its representation of scene, or act, or thought. It is the art of conceptual thought, and is able to portray in the fullest manner and with all the accuracy of language, the conception which forms the subject of the production. Its power over the emotions lies in the facility and accuracy with which it represents scenes and actions and thoughts that simulate actual life. Just as actual experiences of life are productive of sorrow, or joy, or yearning, or exultation, etc., so the feigned experience which literature portrays engenders a rich and varied emotional reaction. By recounting the glory in the life of the hero, or the ignominy of the coward, it can inspire man to noble deeds; by picturing for us the tragedies of life, it can oppress our hearts with sadness; by interesting us in the fortunes of characters whose lot is cast under sunnier skies than our own, it can lighten our cares; by the proper interpretation of life, it can bring both a philosophic calm and a divine content, or it can turn our hearts to prayer and worship by showing the presence and love of God in the world. But the time would fail us to enumerate all the emotions that literature can stimulate and raise to a motive tension. But in all these cases the method by which it acts upon the emotions is the same, viz., by picturing for us in the definite medium of language some concrete representation that simulates the conditions of life as they actually are or as they might be. Here the emotional responses depend directly upon the fulness and the vividness of the portrayal.

Music, on the other hand, as an emotional excitant stands in striking contrast to literature; while it is not less versatile nor less powerful in its emotional effectiveness, it is justly considered as the most vague and indefinite of the arts. It cannot express in its symbolism even the most general outlines of the scenes and actions and thoughts which literature pictures with such fulness and clearness. It has not less power over the emotions, but its method of stimulating them is radically different from the method of literature. *The secret of the versatile power of music over the emotions lies in the fact that the symbolism of music conforms so closely to the dynamics of the emotional consciousness.* Although this is not a recent discovery, it has not for all that been developed or emphasized as its importance deserves. Aristotle, with his keen insight into the secrets of the inner life, adumbrated this thought when he contended that music of all the arts most closely imitated the inner activity of the soul. And Hanslick, whose whole discussion is against the emotional interpretation of music, in answer to the question, "What element of the emotions does music express?" replied promptly and correctly, "Nur das *dynamische* derselben."[1] The difficulty with him is that he does not appreciate the significance of his concession He passes it by as having but little import, when in truth this is the very strongest factor emotionally that could possibly have been named. In granting that music does give the dynamic of the emotions, he

[1] *Vom Musikalisch-Schonen,* p 32

has granted that there must be some very intimate relation between music and the emotions. But just what this relation is, and why it means so much, is yet to be stated.

The musical elements which in their mere sound attributes reflect the dynamic qualities of the emotions, are the same elements that we have had occasion to mention in other connections, viz., modification of Force and Tempo, Movement, Rhythm, the effect of the Major and the Minor modes, as well as the climacteric character of melodic and harmonic progressions. By means of these the musician is able to give in the bare sense attributes of music a very accurate representation of the dynamic qualities of the various emotions. If the emotion is excitatory, consciousness moves with increased speed and a higher tension; this is duplicated in musical symbolism by a quick tempo and greater stress in playing. If the emotion is one of yearning, it is characterized by a serious mental tone, relative slowness of the stream of consciousness and by a feeling of obstruction and hindrance; these can be duplicated in music by a sedate rhythm, a slow tempo, a legato touch, and by the use of the minor mode with its altered and obstructed harmonies. If the feeling tone is cheerful, the mental processes are all healthful and strong, and confidence is a ruling characteristic of the state of mind: music can express just such qualities in sound by an *allegro* movement, and by a firm, confident touch in expressing the sound pattern, whatever it may be. Thus we might continue, and just as far as we could give the dynamic characteristics of the emotions, so far could they be duplicated by means of some of these dynamic qualities of music.

The secret of the emotional value of literature lies in its power of accurate representation of those conditions which in real life would bring such an emotional reaction. In music the same power is gained by duplicating in musical sound the dynamic qualities of the various emotions. The illuminating word therefore in the one case is *representation*, in the other *suggestion*. In music the dynamic elements of the sound, the tempo, the force, the progressions, the rhythm, suggest the mood in which such attributes predominate, and from these mere forms of sensuous stimulus the proper emotion arises and spreads itself over consciousness. Usually the suggestion is not confined to any one of these factors, but several act together and with cumulative effect, so that there is in the mere sound symbolism a compelling power to insure emotions of the proper tone, though no imagery be present to mold the thought. Thus, while we must perforce admit that music is too vague and indefinite in its symbolism to picture forms or scenes so as to control the emotional response as literature does, this does not mean that the emotional interpretation of music is without foundation. There is no art that has a stronger influence over the emotions than music, nor that manifests this power in more varied ways. And this is due in the main to the similarity between the dynamic elements of musical symbolism and the dynamic elements of the emotions which music arouses and stimulates.

3. Music, in the third place, is also remarkable for the power it exerts over the human mind. This power shows itself in two distinct ways: First music is sensuously more clamant, more impressive, more

insistent than any other art. The medium of the art, the objective stimulus, sound has for some reason greater force, engrossing the attention more urgently and completely than the like stimulus of any other art.

Again, the power of music is revealed in the emotions music arouses. No other art, with the possible exception of literature as exemplified in the novel and the drama, takes hold of the emotional consciousness with such compelling force. In its influence over the emotions music has direct, dramatic power. As a pure form of art, that is, in its structural, formal qualities, and in the exemplification of the higher æsthetic attributes, music does not differ essentially from the other arts. Such qualities wherever found produce a deep, contemplative, almost passive reaction. But in its impressive, dramatic qualities music is unique and demands, therefore, some explanation for its power.

There are three points to be mentioned as throwing light upon the power of music. First, the biological significance of sound, the medium in which music is expressed; second, the organic character of rhythm, always an indispensable element in music; and third, the dynamic character of the elements of musical symbolism.

As an art, music gains greatly in impressiveness and in power by reason of the fact that it has for its medium of expression that sense stimulus which both psychologists and biologists are telling us is most intimately connected with the emotional life. An Italian psychologist only recently, seeking for an explanation of the close relation between sound stimuli and the emotions, has advanced the theory that the fibres of the auditory and the pneumogastric nerves are closely interlaced; thus the stimulation of the auditory nerve affects also the vital organs controlled by the latter nerve, and this in turn affects the emotional consciousness. It is true that this hypothesis has not been verified, but the fact it was meant to explain is too obvious to be questioned.

More illuminating is the explanation of biologists. They, too, impressed with the fact that sound seems most intimately connected with the emotions, have not ceased to remind us, from the time of Darwin and Spencer, that sound is the most natural, the most common and the most effective way of expressing and communicating the emotions, not only for man, but for the lower animals as well. Having become fixed as the habitual method of emotional expression, sound is sensuously the most exciting form of sense stimulus used in art. Spencer's theory of music, it will be remembered, was that music is but a development from the emotional outcries of our primitive ancestors. Here again we leave theorists in peace to work out and to justify their hypotheses; but the point we are interested to make is even here further justified. They give an impartial, unbiased judgment and withal a truth that goes far to explain the attributes of music we are discussing.

Common experience also confirms our point; the moans of a sufferer excite our sympathy and pity as a sight of his emaciated form will not; animals, habitually silent, in extremities of suffering or terror give utterance to cries of the most expressive anguish; the importance of inflection and accent by the actor or the reader in producing the emotional response from the listener also calls attention to the expressiveness of sound as mere sound. Thus, through the long development of the ages sound qualities have become indissolubly associated with emotional states and have come to be the most exciting, the most powerful sense stimulus in producing emotional reactions.

This natural impressiveness of sound, instilled and fixed in us by ages of development in which issues of life and death were involved, is carried over from the realm of man's normal experience with the world to the realm of music, and there functions with its pristine significance unimpaired and not greatly altered. Here it manifests itself by giving to the mere sound qualities of music harmonic factors such as harmony, discord, dissonance, and the effect of the major and minor modes, timbre, and modifications of tempo and force an influence over the emotions that is almost hypnotic in its directness and power. The secret of this influence, then, to state it in other terms, lies in the inherited tendency to rely chiefly upon sound attributes in interpreting the emotional content of the mental experience of others. Through heredity this tendency has become fixed, until it is both natural and inevitable to regard modification of sound as the most direct and unmistakable evidence of the feeling tone of others.

We have already had occasion to call attention to the organic character of rhythm and to state in what sense this expression is to be understood. So far as can now be seen, it is due to the metabolism, purely physiological changes, of the nerve cells. The accumulation of energy there is approximately uniform, while the nervous discharge is essentially explosive, a certain potential being required to overcome the internal resistance of the nerve fibres. Under such conditions the discharge must necessarily be periodic or rhythmical. If this be the true explanation of rhythm, it follows that rhythm considered from the mental side is an instinctive mode of reaction. This means much when translated into terms of impellant force. In proportion as an act is instinctive, that is, structurally and functionally provided for in the economy of the organism, the driving force, the *vis a tergo*, to be effective must be the stronger. The *leading* force of consciousness is in such cases inoperative, the power all-impellant. By means of discipline and education and by taking advantage of instincts of later development, man can place rational motives, high moral ideals, over primitive instincts, but without such training and years of external inhibition, instincts by their native strength would determine the actions of man as well as of the lower animals. The impulse to play in the child is naturally stronger than the impulse to work; the desire for wealth, the acquisitive instinct, even in spite of years of training, is sometimes stronger than the cultivated habit of social regard. Education is easy both for teacher and pupil just so far as educational practice can base itself upon these motor proclivities, and a ceaseless struggle so far as some must be opposed. When we say therefore that rhythm is organic, we say it is instinctive and ascribe to it all the clamant strength that belongs to these inherited predispositions to certain forms of motor reactions. It may be blind and unreflective and without any consciousness of its true function, but it is clamant, intense and strong.

Our third point, the dynamic character of the elements of musical symbolism, has been touched upon in explaining the versatility of music; but it is not less effective as one of the sources of the power which is also characteristic of music. As the principle has been stated, it affirms that music gains greatly in power by virtue of the fact that the elements of its symbolism are inherently dynamic. Thus there are, even in the sense stimulus itself, the strongest suggestions of force and movement, and these through heredity have became the natural excitants of the emotions. If we pause for a moment to enumerate what have been called the sensuous or impressive elements of music, it will be readily seen how strong in them all is this dynamic factor. Rhythm is surcharged with movement and energy and is, indeed, meaningless without them. Both the movement of the rhythmic sequence, and the accent by which rhythm is marked, are due in the last analysis to the expenditure of energy. And this is evident, not merely in the broader psychological interpretation, but even in the sense stimulus itself. Modifications of tempo and force are inseparable from movement and change, both dynamic factors.

And even timbre and harmony are so intimately connected with the progression of melody that they too give the impression of being charged with the same dynamic power. Music, therefore, we see, is inseparable from movement. Gurney calls melody "Ideal Motion." The deep psychological significance of this fact will be better appreciated if we compare music in this respect with the other arts.

The purpose of the painter, for example, is to choose some critical moment in the experience of his characters, or some scene, and to crystallize this moment for us in such a way that the sense qualities will be pleasing and the thought content expressive of some phase of life. But he is limited by the con-

ditions of his art to the representation of a single moment. In all the forms of his art, in landscape, in
portraiture, in *genre* painting, this condition is absolute. There is, therefore, a total absence of any real
dynamic element in the sense stimulus. In this
sense of the term all painting is "still-life." It is
true that painting has its figures representing motion and energy and effort; but even here there is
wanting that real movement and action in the sense
stimulus which is so characteristic of music. In
Millet's "Sower," for example, the figure is replete
with energy and action, but the mere sense effect in
strength is distinctly below the effect of a strong
rhythm, or the effect of modified force or a changed
tempo. When the painter has done all in his power
the feeling of movement and energy is still *but in-
ferential*, not a direct datum of sense. In this art
there are only quiescent figures, unchanging color
forms.

The influence of these facts upon the mental reaction is important; since there is no similarity
dynamically between the sense factors and the natural life of the emotions, the feeling is aroused not
through the suggestiveness of the sense factors, but
chiefly through the appreciation of the thought content. And while there may be a gain in purity and
in accuracy, there is a distinct loss in force. A painting because of this static quality of the sense stimulus
tends to keep the emotion aroused upon one unchanging plane, rather than to develop it up to its
climax according to the natural developing phases
of a feeling state. Once I comprehend the artist's
thought and appreciate his technique, there is nothing in the stimulus itself to carry the emotions on to a

richer, fuller life. But the emotions are naturally climacteric, dramatic, and require definite and developing antecedents to arouse them to their greatest depth and to their greatest strength. Compare, if you wish an example of this, the emotional effect of reading an account of a death as given in our newspapers and the tragic death of Hamlet. In the first case we know nothing of the antecedents of the death, which may be fully as tragic as that of Hamlet, while in the latter we are led up to the death which comes as a climax to a long, emotional and dramatic sequence of events. The one is a mere expression of a fact, a sad fact doubtless; but the other, in giving us a connected account of the circumstances, prepares us for the full emotional reaction.

In viewing a painting with its static and momentary conception, the emotions which have been aroused by the representation tend at once, by a well-known law of mental fatigue, to fade away. The stimulus does not develop. It is true that through association the representation may be so enriched that the emotions will develop and be carried on to a full and a rich reaction. The associated factors and the strength of the subjective element will provide for this. The point we wish to make is not that such works of art do not stimulate the emotions, but that they do not do so so effectively as music. In the case of painting the emotions are aroused principally through the meaning attached to the representation, that is, through the thought content, but in the case of music by this and also by the suggestion in the dynamic factors of the sense stimulus itself.

The exceptional power which certain forms of literature exert upon the human mind, e. g., the novel and the drama, well confirm our point as a positive example of the principles which give music its power. As Lessing long ago explained, literature is peculiarly adapted to express ideas in which there is development from moment to moment. It conforms to the natural process of thought and so is adapted to express thought relations. Literature, therefore, is to be classed with music as an art adapted to carry the mind on to emotional climaxes of great intensity and force. By means of conceptual representations presented in logical or panoramic succession, that is, by the concrete imagery of language picture, or by certain thoughts, the emotions are awakened and stimulated and carried on through a natural order of development to maximum degrees of intensity. Literature, like music, takes a deep hold upon the mind because it conforms closely to the natural functioning of the emotional consciousness. Unlike painting, it does not leave to the individual the task of mentally completing the drama suggested, but carries it out definitely so that if the listener but follows the imagery presented he can hardly help but become engrossed in the story and follow emotionally all the changes and vicissitudes of its characters.

But even as compared with literature, music in one respect stands superior; the dynamic similarity of literature to the emotional life is confined chiefly to the thought content, in music it extends even to the elements of its sensuous expression. And we are still functionally so truly bodily that these sensuous elements have an amazing hold upon us emotionally. It is man's life-long task so to become master of himself that he can subordinate in certain matters of moral import the instinctive to the rational, the sensuous to the intellectual. Music in its symbolism, both in the thought content expressed and in its sensuous factors employed, conforms closely to the natural laws of emotional reactions. This symbolism therefore makes a direct and a tremendous appeal to the emotional consciousness. Thus it is that music ranks in power with the most powerful forms of the literary art, and in some respects surpasses it in the directness and immediacy of its appeal.

CHAPTER IX

THE CONTENT OF MUSIC

1. The central problem in the philosophy of an art is the problem of its *content*. What is the essential nature of its subject matter, its inner core of thought, the irreducible substratum that gives it character and determines its proper function in the economy of life? This is the inquiry that goes nearest to the heart of the matter, that lays bare as it were the very principles of its being. In comparison with this subject the problem of *form* is relatively simple and easy. The truth there sought can be empirically investigated and scientifically determined, but the data thus gained are only the starting-point for the more profound inquiry concerning the content. However, though the problem is difficult, its solution will yield ample returns for all the labor expended; for when once determined, the content becomes a very touchstone through which that art may be related to other phases of human experience.

It is upon this problem of the content of music, it will be remembered, that musical theorists have long been divided into two opposing schools—the " Formalists " and the " Expressionists." The former contend that the content of music is nothing more than the auditory nerve receives and transmits to the brain, that is, sound patterns, melodic, harmonic and rhythmic, and withal as a stimulus sensuously pleasing, and in their mere sonorous reality beautiful. This school, therefore, emphasizes the architectonic, the formal attributes of music, finding the essence of the beauty of music, the content, in the mere formal play of tones and in the structural unity expressed in musical symbols. The latter, on the other hand, contend for the emotional significance of music, finding its true function not merely or principally in the play of tones standing in logical relations to one another, but in the stimulation of the emotions. The one school considers music merely an "arabesque of sound," the other a "language of the emotions."

This wide divergence of opinion is due largely to the two points of view from which musical theorists have considered the question. The theories, therefore, are not necessarily mutually exclusive nor irreconcilable. The Formalists, considering music from the objective standpoint, describe it in terms of its objective reality, that is, music consists of sound patterns of definite logical form, differing in their rhythmic, melodic and harmonic attributes. Being an objective phenomenon, its ultimate reality must be ascertained through the sense. That this is a valid and a legitimate point of view cannot be denied. The inadequacy of this conception of music is not due to any falsity in the general tenets held, but rather to the fact that the whole truth can no more be gained from one point of view than a solid can be seen in its entirety from any one side. So long as the standpoint of the Formalists is rigidly maintained their argument is well-nigh if not quite irrefragable. Music is certainly all that they claim it to be, though not necessarily merely that: it *is* a well-ordered, logical sequence of pleasing musical sounds express-

ing a musical thought. Certainly it is. But it may
be all this and much more besides.

The indictment to be brought against this hypothesis therefore is not so much *inaccuracy* as *inadequacy*.
To limit the term *content* merely to that which is seen
from the objective point of view, is to use the term in
the most superficial and unphilosophic manner. Observe the illuminating analogy that can be drawn in
this respect between music and the other arts! The
content of sculpture is not the bare form of stone to
be apprehended by the eye alone. The content of
painting is not the mere form on the canvas, the color,
the light and shade, the drawing, the composition and
perspective, qualities visible to the eye. These are
all essential qualities of painting, it is true; but
granted that they are worth all that painters claim,
even so we do not fathom the depth of art or find the
true secret of artistic genius. Who beholding the
Sistine Madonna would be content to note merely
the form, the lines, the shading, the color, and not
feel the influence of the pure, thoughtful soul that
looks out of the wondering eyes of the Child's
mother? And if there are paintings whose value
lies wholly in the formal attributes, as there doubtless are, it is due rather to the limitations of genius
than to the adequacy of the theory itself. They who
painted thus lacked the genius of Raphael and Angelo and those who reveal in their works the deeper
passions and truths of life This latter is the sublime
in art, the deeper content that not only satisfies the
soul of the beholder, but even the quest of the philosopher looking for the deep foundations of life and
of art. Who, I say, who has once felt the force and
depth of this element in art, can escape the feeling of

trivialities when he is recalled to the mere sense qualities of art? And yet such an one is he who sees in
music nothing more than a discourse of sweet sounds.
The objective elements of every art are genuine and
important, and with their principles and sensuous
beauty worthy of intelligent appreciation. But after
all they are but the means of expressing a thought
that can hardly be found in such an analysis as this.
Music, as has been shown throughout our whole discussion, has its thought and its emotional aspects as
well as its striking sense attributes. When we refer
to the content of music, therefore, we must comprehend under the term something more than is found
in the conception of the Formalist.

2. From the subjective point of view, the standpoint of the Expressionists, the time-honored question is, "Does music express the emotions?" This
question they answer unhesitatingly and emphatic-
ally in the affirmative. Music is not only able to express the emotions, but so direct is its power over the
emotional consciousness that it is, as it were, a very
language of the emotions. But the question itself is
most unfortunately stated because of the manifest
ambiguity in the pivotal word "express." And besides it no longer serves to state accurately the real
problem in musical æsthetics. Few indeed are they
who still hold to a strict interpretation of the Formalistic hypothesis and deny to music a direct and a
powerful influence over the emotional consciousness.
In this respect the Expressionists have won a deci-
sive victory. The real, vital problem in musical
æsthetics to-day is the problem of the relative value
of the emotional and the intellectual elements in
music, it being no longer denied that music does

contain them both. The result of our psychological analysis justifies this new point of attack. We leave the old question, therefore, and turn to this more modern and more fruitful inquiry.

3. In an inquiry as to the emotional significance of music, it will be well to keep in mind a distinction that has been suggested between the *dramatic* or *impressive* attributes of music and its more comprehensive, more abstract, æsthetic qualities. No small part of the confusion in which the subject of musical æsthetics now stands is due to a failure to distinguish properly between the impressive qualities of musical sound considered merely as sound and the more truly æsthetic qualities of music which make it a true form of art. As one writer expresses the distinction: "Music presents two sets of psychological phenomena. It can suggest and stimulate feelings akin to those produced by the vicissitudes of real life; and it can interest, fascinate, delight or weary and displease by what we can only call the purely musical qualities of its sound patterns. Music thus awakens two sets of emotions—a dramatic one referred to its expressiveness, and an æsthetic one correlated with the presence or absence of beauty." [1] The distinction is an excellent one and our discussion of the emotional significance of music will be based upon it. Music, by the presence of certain factors, is peculiarly adapted to arouse and to stimulate the emotions in a direct and dramatic way; but it is also by the presence of universal æsthetic qualities capable of arousing the less intense æsthetic emotions or sentiments.

As an art, music is blessed with unique power and

Vernon Lee, *Riddle of Music*, Quarterly Review, Jan., 1906.

effectiveness by having as its medium of expression that sense stimulus which both for biological and psychological reasons is most directly and intensely impressive. Consequently there is to music, by virtue of the character of its medium, an impressiveness strong enough at times to overbalance completely the less obtrusive, less clamant æsthetic qualities which belong to music in its higher artistic relations. These impressive or dramatic qualities of musical sound are all so perfectly adapted to awaken and to stimulate the emotions that it seems to be playing loose with the facts in the case to explain them in any other way.

But besides the impressiveness of musical sound due to evolutionary factors, music exemplifies as a true form of art certain æsthetic attributes common to all the arts and universally regarded as principles of beauty in its purer forms. These principles, we say, are common to all the arts; the musician, like the poet or the painter, has an idea to express in sensuous form, an idea characterized by certain assignable æsthetic principles due to the character of the idea and not to the nature of the medium in which it is expressed. That the idea is musical, not conceptual or pictorial, in no way alters this fundamental fact. Because such an idea is musical and must be expressed in musical sounds, it has its own characteristic sense qualities; these are the obvious factors that first appeal to the natural ear, the *differentia* determining its specie.

But if the composition is worthy of the name of *art* there must be besides these pleasing qualities of sound, or behind them, an idea exemplifying, notwithstanding its musical character, the same æsthetic ideals and principles that determine the value of any other work of art. Indeed, music is an *art* only by virtue of this fact. Art is something deeper, something nobler and more significant than mere sense stimulus, enriched and intensified though it be by all the qualities that can be predicated of such forms of objective reality. Music is music, if you please, because of its sound attributes, but it is an art only because it is a vehicle for the expression of thought. These thought attributes are the principles that determine its *genus*, that is, make it a true form of art.

But in whatever terms it is stated, the distinction is valid and important and much will be gained toward a truer conception of music if it is kept constantly before us. In discussing the emotional significance of music, therefore, we shall observe this twofold character of music and note first some of the impressive qualities of musical sound, and then some of the most typical æsthetic principles.

4. It is no difficult task to analyze a musical composition so as to determine the various sources of its psychological effect. Indeed so few and so simple are these elements found to be that they have been declared for this very reason inadequate for the demands made upon them by the Expressionist's hypothesis. We need not hesitate, therefore, to enumerate them the real problem is to understand how factors apparently so simple can still be so tremendously effective. Gurney, in his *Power of Sound*, enumerates the following means at the disposal of the musician, whereby he is able to awaken emotional responses in the minds of his hearers: Timbre, the use of the Major and the Minor Modes, Harmonic Features such as Discords and Resolutions, Pace, strongly

marked Rhythmic Outlines and Undecided Rhythm.[1]
To these must be added, certainly, modifications of
Force. These dramatic or impressive factors can
all be conveniently subsumed under the following
heads: Rhythm, Harmonic Factors including the
major and the minor modes, Timbre, and modifications in Force and in Tempo.

It is little wonder that to those of a formalistic disposition of mind these few elements, one and all,
should seem too vague, too indefinite to meet the requirements of a "language of the emotions." Moreover, the emotions are notoriously averse to any
orderly manipulation such as the term "language"
implies. But while this is all true, we may still inquire as to the presence and value of the emotional
element in music.

Rhythm has already been declared to be instinctive, that is, directly, and without the mediation of
consciousness, impressive and emotional. The reaction it calls forth is *quasi*-reflex, but with the most
profound and dramatic influence over the emotional
consciousness. This point needs no further elucidation.

Harmonic elements also have a direct, sensuous,
dramatic power as well as a more complex, æsthetic
significance. While the explanation of the major
and the minor modes, for example, entails an abstract
analysis and shows the presence of complex psychological principles, these principles manifest their
presence chiefly in the reaction to the mere sensuous
differences so emphasized in Helmholtz's explanation. The contrasted effect of the two modes, therefore, is also more direct, dramatic, than an intel-

[1] *Vid.* Chapter XIV.

lectual appreciation of all the elements shown by a logical analysis to be involved. And this mental response also is strongly colored emotionally.

Of the same nature and due to the same developmental reasons is the effect of discords and resolutions mentioned by Gurney. They also are potent emotionally, but the reaction to them has become so habitual that the reflective element, if it was ever present, has been lost, and they are appreciated now in this same *quasi*-instinctive fashion, and for their emotional value.

Timbre or "tone-color," as it is often called, refers to the *quality* of the sound, due, as physicists tell us, to the presence and prominence of various overtones entering into the composition of the fundamental tone. This tone-quality is also directly and dramatically impressive, that is, has in itself emotional significance. The recognition of this fact is not a discovery of modern music. Aristotle in his scheme of education, because of the dissolute tendency of such instruments, would interdict the flute, the harp, and the lyre.[1] But it is only in recent years, through the development of orchestration, that this fact has been seized upon and developed so as to produce a new departure in music. In the light of the recognition and emphasis it is thus receiving, it will be well to note carefully its true character and thus to see the strength and the weakness of the movement based upon it.

We have just said that timbre is a quality of sound due primarily to the character of the overtones produced by various instruments or voices. Because of the different shapes of the resonating

[1] *Vid Politics*, Bk. VIII.

cavities of musical instruments the fundamental tones have different overtones, or these are variously emphasized. Thus timbre is primarily a sensuous attribute, and to pitch and intensity and "touch" is added another sense attribute hardly less obvious than the most evident of these sensuous qualities of sound. To a close observer it is not strange that a characteristic so palpable as this should be used to base a new departure in music; its inherent importance justifies the movement.

Timbre thus is the principle underlying the decided musical movement of our day, viz., *orchestration*. To discuss this subject in detail is the work of the musician; we shall only note its principles. In the orchestra, as we know it to-day, there are certain groups of instruments, each group characterized by its own quality of tone. Such, for example, are the "strings," the "wood-wind," the "brass" and the "battery." But the principle leads to a much more extended division than this; indeed, each instrument of each group has its own peculiar color, and for the musician this has a certain specific value. Each instrument, therefore, is an opportunity for the musician to further accentuate this sensuous character of musical sound, and to make a direct appeal to the emotions of the listener. The *insistent* tones of the violin, the *martial* tone of the brass, the plaintive tone of the flute, the clanging cymbal, illustrate what is meant. And even between instruments as closely related as the violin and the viola the modern world has learned to ascribe important differences.

The modern school of "colorists," seizing upon these qualitative distinctions in conjunction with the other sense qualities, have developed them most fertilely and have produced a music of unprecedented intensity and passion. Strauss, for example, in some of his latest "tone-poems" has startled, amazed and even shocked the musical world by the passion he pictures. Whether or not this be the highest or even the truest form of art, there is no question of its dramatic effectiveness. The thought will rise, however, that in the very intensity of his music and in the appeal he makes to these sensuous attributes he is departing from the sober advance along the lines of pure musical thought, rather than pointing with unerring hand to the sacred way of enduring art. To ignore the demands of pure thought for the greater impressiveness of sense is, in all art and for all time, a questionable procedure. However, this is no reason why the movement may not result, when sober second thought has pruned away its asperities, in a decided enrichment of the musical art, not only in an increased sensuous beauty and effectiveness, but also in the possibilities for working out new thought relations.

To complete the list of these impressive or dramatic attributes of musical sound, we refer again to modifications of Force and of Tempo, which, because of their similarity dynamically to emotional changes, have a direct and a powerful suggestibility. They too are made use of in modern music to heighten and intensify its sensuous effect, and belong, therefore, to the same category as the factors previously mentioned.

In considering the character and mental significance of these factors, the first common attribute is their immediacy. As has been pointed out, they may all be regarded as attributes of the musical tones considered as sound; they do not therefore depend for their effect upon their symbolic content, though they may all have such value, but as mere modifications of sensuous stimuli have the directness and force of sensational and perceptual elements. It is a well-known psychological law that factors long and repeatedly used assume a *quasi*-reflex character, exercising their pristine function without the mediation of consciousness. This is just the case with the factors we are now discussing. Once interpreted as symbols of emotional reaction, they have now become fixed in the organic structure of the individual and function with their primal force, but without consciousness of the end they subserve.

Another common attribute of these sense qualities is their indefiniteness. Were any further evidence needed to show the inadequacy of the expressionistic hypothesis, this fact should prove convincing. The sensuous factors, remarkable though they be, are one and all too vague, too indefinite to fulfil the exigencies of a language. And yet as compared with the other arts, music is in this direction far superior to any art that might be named. The sensuous factors utilized for emotional expressiveness in sculpture, or architecture, or in literature, or even in painting, are not to be compared with those available in music, either in number or in expressiveness. So, while we admit their conceptual vagueness, we must not overlook their sensuous suggestibility. And as we have already said, not accurate representation, but suggestibility, is the illuminating term in the psychology of the emotions.

In the net outcome upon the emotional consciousness I am not sure but that this indefiniteness is a distinct gain rather than a source of weakness. For example, if I am reading a poem or looking at a picture I must follow the representation there definitely and accurately expressed. Such representations may or they may not be for me rich in interest and in emotional significance: that will depend upon my education and previous experience. But the indefinite suggestibility of the sensuous factors of music leaves the mind free to create its own imagery, to bring to consciousness ideas which for it are fraught with feeling. The laws of association teach that it may be just for this reason, indeed, that they are revived. So long as these factors have character enough to give color to the feeling, and this cannot be denied, their conceptual vagueness may therefore be a distinct gain emotionally, not a source of weakness. Such being the case, it is folly to overlook their inherent character and to deny that, psychologically considered, they have direct and remarkable emotional significance. Being direct and sensuous, they serve to give to the emotions music engenders a warmth and vividness and color that approximates in these particulars the emotions produced by the vicissitudes of real life.

5. In estimating the value of the emotional element in music, the more abstract æsthetic attributes must also be considered. Though they are by no means so clamant or exciting or so dramatically powerful as the sensuous qualities to which we have already called attention, they are the source of an æsthetic pleasure, pale in hue it may be, but pure in texture. Such, for example, are unity, symmetry, gracefulness, originality, and the like. As æsthetic attributes they are common to all the arts, though in the case

of each differently expressed, the unity in a drama is not produced by the same means as the unity in a building or in a painting, or in a musical composition. Nevertheless, since it is unity in each case, the psychological reaction is identical. So far as the logical and psychological value of the principle is concerned, it is a matter of indifference whether it is manifested in one work of art or in another. The emotional value of these æsthetic attributes, when realized in music, therefore, is not different from their psychological function when found in any of the other arts; it is true that their effect is supplemented, often overshadowed, by the more striking effect of the dramatic qualities of musical sound, but as æsthetic principles, considered for their own sake, there is no sufficient ground for introducing a distinction

These æsthetic attributes in music, as in the other arts, produce the characteristic æsthetic emotion, an emotion of a refined, intellectual character, calm or contemplative, but pure, and recognized as of high inherent worth. They and they alone redeem music from being merely an effective means of emotional stimulation, and place it high in the category of art. Thus the emotions they arouse are an indispensable element in the psychological reaction to music; otherwise, there is nothing worthy the name of art.

The conclusion, therefore, to which we are led by the argument, is that if the proper function of art in its other forms is to awaken an emotional reaction, the same is true of music, and also to a like degree. The purpose of art is one, whatever its form. Music is blessed by having at its disposal, due to the medium in which it is expressed, numerous factors of direct emotional significance; but these in no way change its function as a form of art. They give it power, they give it universality, they give it versatility; but the true purpose of music is not changed thereby, and any attempt to neglect the former or to even emphasize the latter is a departure from the true pathway of art and of art development.

6. In our discussion of the intellectual element in music, the purpose of this chapter does not demand that we enter into a detailed description of such factors, but only that we attempt to *evaluate* them. In the true content of music is there a real and a vital intellectual factor ? Or, in other words, in the æsthetic experience resulting from the appreciation of a musical composition, what is the value of the intellectual activity involved ?

As a preliminary to the consideration of this subject, it should be remembered that there is the widest difference in musical compositions as to the presence and relative importance of these intellectual elements. Some compositions depend for their effect so largely upon the dramatic qualities and so little upon formal architectonic elements, that they are correctly characterized as emotional; others subordinate these attributes and demand upon the part of the listener a very keen, analytic attitude of mind if the content is to be at all adequately apprehended. In the first case, appeal is made largely to reflex and instinctive factors, and the mind is more passively receptive than discriminatingly and actively analytic. But there is music also that cannot be comprehended in any such listless fashion. The compositions of Bach or

Beethoven, for example, or of any of the classical composers, demand a marshalling of the powers of the mind and a critical and sustained attention that can be denominated nothing else than intellectual. In this respect music is again closely analogous to various forms of literature. Just as some poems, for example, require little more than a passive though sensitive response to the obvious imagery of the word pictures, so some music is adequately apprehended through a simple response to its dramatic elements. But there is literature also which, to be appreciated, requires the most energetic activity of the mind's analytic powers and of intellectual synthesis. In the latter case, the proper æsthetic emotion comes only through the clear comprehension of the thought.

When we speak of the intellectual element in music, therefore, it is evident that we do not refer to any fixed or constant factor. Some music is rich in such elements, some relies for its effect more upon the impressive attributes of musical sound. Under such conditions we can escape the difficulty either by making our remarks so general that they will apply to the two extremes, or we can inquire more specifically as to the general character of the intellectual processes involved in the musical experience, and then determine the source of the pleasure in such activity. Our method will be the latter one. Two questions will serve to focalize our remarks: First, what are the intellectual processes involved in apprehending a musical composition? And, second, do such activities result in a truly æsthetic pleasure?

In apprehending a musical composition as an

objective form, there are involved necessarily all those activities of the sense organ and brain centres used in any perceptual process. This is obviously true,. whether the composition be of the emotional or of the intellectual type. It makes no difference, so far as this stage of the process is concerned, whether the composition is to be apprehended for æsthetic or for critical or for scientific purposes. There must be a certain voluntary or involuntary focussing of the attention, a real though an unreflective discrimination of factors, an implicit or explicit judgment such as is involved in any process of sense perception. However, this does not get to the heart of the matter, for the æsthetic experience is determined, not by the process of sense perception, but by the mental attitude toward an object when perceived. We must look, therefore, to the processes involved in the apprehension of these higher æsthetic qualities of a work of art.

In the æsthetic apprehension and appreciation of a quality like *unity*, intellectual processes of a high order are involved. The unity of a musical composition is not a datum of sense, and thus a part of the perceptual process. If the composition is at all complex, it is more like the unity of a drama or a novel, an attribute to be recognized only as sense data are analyzed and the relation of part to part intelligently understood. To be more specific, the recognition of unity in music worthy of the name of art, presupposes an analysis of the composition into its structural elements and the recognition of the relation between them, the evaluation consciously or unconsciously of thematic, rhythmic and harmonic features, and the whole series of related elements synthesized into an artistic whole. It is true that for a mere impressionistic appreciation of some music all this need not be done in so clear cut and conscious a fashion as is implied in our remarks; there is what we may call an *emotional unity* attainable through the dramatic qualities of musical sound. But for a composition built upon more severe intellectual lines, this kind of mental reaction will not suffice.

The reason classical music is so often a bore to the average listener is exactly the same as the reason technical discussions fail to interest the man on the street; he is unacquainted with the terminology in which the thought is expressed and fails, therefore, to find meaning in the sounds through which the thought is expressed.

The recognition and appreciation of balance or symmetry in a composition implies a high degree of refinement in discriminating ability and enough practice to lead to the appreciation of contrasted musical elements.

Strength in expression, we have said, implies comprehensiveness and clearness of vision, that is to say, a logical, masterful understanding of the thought expressed. This is essentially an intellectual process, a matter of the understanding, not of the emotions.

The detection and appreciation of gracefulness is first of all a sensibility for fine distinctions, both of sense and of thought, and is, so far, closely akin to the other intellectual processes of discrimination and judgment.

For the appreciation of originality and significance in the content of a composition, there is required the

functioning of the mind in the most abstract and
plainly intellectual way These two attributes are
inherently attributes of thought, not of the emotions,
and can be apprehended and appreciated, therefore,
only through the activity of intellect. That this
is true will be readily seen if it is remembered what
the recognition of such attributes implies, viz., the
analysis of the most abstract ideas, the application
of standards of intellectual and emotional values,
and comparisons with ideas and ideals which are
comparable with the abstract processes of scientific
judgment and reasoning.

We conclude, therefore, that music of any real
artistic value, because such music must exemplify
these various æsthetic attributes, does contain an
intellectual as well as an emotional element. Thus
pure emotionalism as the basis for a theory of music is proven inadequate. Not only are intellectual
elements present, but they play so large a part in
the musical experience that they must be recognized as an indispensable element in the musical experience. With this conclusion forced upon us, the
question now arises, is such intellectual activity for
its own sake, or for the sake of the pleasure resulting
therefrom ?

To maintain that these intellectual processes
exist for their own sake were to confuse the æsthetic
and the scientific experience. We affirm at once,
therefore, and without further argument, that they
are not to be thus interpreted. But, on the other
hand, the analogy between the musical experience
and other forms of artistic reaction leads us to
assert that in the intellectual activity involved in
the apprehension of these æsthetic attributes there

is that refined, intellectual pleasure known as the characteristic æsthetic emotion. To explain why such intellectual activity should give pleasure, we shall refer, in lieu of a better one, to the biological theory of pleasure and its function.

If there is an æsthetic pleasure in the physiological activity of the sense organs, due, as the theory phrases it, "to the healthful functioning of the organs involved," the presumption is that pleasure of a similar character would result, as the mind in its higher processes functions æsthetically. Indeed, if the theory is to be credible at all, it must be so. Pleasure is the reward Nature gives her children for working for their own advantage, pain her penalty for self-injury. But the intellect, evolutionists tell us, is Nature's crowning gift to man, the most perfect instrument of adaptation and adjustment. Since, however, the mind is still the battle field of evolutionary forces, favorable activities still need the preferential accompaniment of pleasure. Thus we are justified by the theory in regarding these higher intellectual processes involved in the æsthetic experience as productive of a pleasurable emotion, strong enough, unless inhibited by other stronger factors, to insure a preference for such modes of activity. Thus, ultimately, even these most pronounced intellectual processes involved in the highest type of musical experience yield a rich return in the common currency of the art realm, viz., in the emotions. We close the chapter with a brief summary.

7. The analysis of this chapter has been based upon the distinction between the sensuous qualities of musical sound and the more abstract æsthetic attributes of music which give it place in the category

of art. These sensuous attributes of music psychologically considered have greater value than the sensuous attributes of any other art. So urgent are
they, so clamant, so intense in their appeal, that they
tend to overshadow the more intellectual attributes
with which they have been contrasted. In the course
of men's development these sensuous factors have
acquired a direct and a powerful influence over the
emotional consciousness. Music, therefore, that
relies chiefly for its effect upon such attributes,
whether it be the crude music of primitive people or
"popular music," or much of the music of the romanticists, or the "tone-poems" of the current
movement, is as to its content predominately emotional. Such music may be tremendously impressive and intense, and yet demand but little intellectual activity or appreciation.

On the other hand, there is music that produces its
proper effect not so much through the use of these
impressive attributes as through the elaboration of
pure musical thought. So little are the mere sense
factors regarded, so important is the presentation of
the thought for its own sake, that a failure to appreciate this latter element results inevitably in boredom
for the listener, none the less real that it is unfash-
ionable to let it be known. In music of this class the
content is *musical thought* expressed for its own sake,
thought demanding upon the part of the listener
concentrated attention and genuine intellectual
labor. And, yet, even here the emotional element is
not absent, for it is through such intellectual activity
that the purest and richest æsthetic emotion is to be
gained.

Because there are these two well-defined aspects to
music, and because they are utilized in such varying

proportions, the content of music cannot be expressed solely in terms of either. Music that employs in the main these impressive attributes of sense, derives its value chiefly from the active functioning of the emotional consciousness. The danger in such music is that it will sacrifice refinement for intensity, a true æsthetic enjoyment for an exciting emotional reaction. However, these factors have their proper place and function in music of the highest type, although alone they are not sufficient.

Music of the sort that will live and be loved perennially, that does not grow old, that tries to stimulate the mind not merely effectively but æsthetically, must do so by finding its virtue principally in these æsthetic attributes. The sensuous attributes, one and all, may then be present to add intensity and warmth and life to further the effect of these more intellectual qualities. But without the latter all the impressiveness, all the intensity, all the dramatic power, will but go to show how sadly the composer has missed the true purpose and function of art. The reason there is any more question as to the content of music than of any other art is due partly, doubtless, to the non-conceptual character of musical symbolism, but also partly to the remarkable emotional impressiveness of these sensuous factors. However, they alone are not sufficient to produce masterpieces in this art. Not strength, but refinement of feeling is the true criterion of the æsthetic experience. And this in its greatest purity and beauty can be obtained only in these æsthetic attributes. The future of music, therefore, we dare to say, does not lie in the conception of strongly impressionistic "tone-poems," but in the expression of clear, logical, artistic musical thought.

CHAPTER X

MUSICAL CRITICISM

1. It is not our purpose in this chapter to trespass on the rights of the musical critic by offering suggestions as to the canons of correct musical taste, but rather to get down beneath such canons to examine the principles upon which they rest and by virtue of which they have authority Musical criticism being a systematic evaluation of individual compositions, it is not surprising if our analysis of music should throw some light also upon the subject of musical values. Whether or not this presumption is justified the discussion itself will decide.

The need for a critical examination into the grounds of musical criticism is particularly urgent. In no other branch of art criticism is there less unanimity of opinion, or so little understanding of the philosophical basis upon which correct judgment must be founded. Musical criticism to-day lacks both system and authority, and the difficulty evidently is that there is no common and philosophical basis for judgment as to what is valuable in music. Consequently individual caprice and multifarious opinions are left to flaunt themselves where there should be unanimity and authority It is not long since one of our leading comic papers amused itself and its readers by publishing side by side a long list of contradictory opinions concerning the value of certain musical productions, taken from the musical criticism of the leading papers of the metropolis of our country.

That musical criticism is in a sad plight no one realizes better than musical critics themselves. Only a few months ago the writer read with interest from the pen of one of the leading critics of the country a jeremiad upon the lamentably unstable condition of musical criticism. That conditions are as they are is due to the failure to get down beneath individual opinion and caprice to the fundamental principles upon which there can be general agreement. When such a starting-point is found, then and then only can musical criticism firmly establish itself for systematic and effective work. It is true that there will always be room for difference in the final judgment, but that is no objection, provided good reasons based upon some tangible principle can be shown. So long as such principles are wanting, however, musical criticism must remain in its present purely individualistic state, a condition not unlike the condition mathematics would be in without its axioms, or science without its postulates.

That there are such principles, provided they can only be found, is as certain as that music is a true form of art, and that art has its own definite characteristics and attributes. If there are principles of literary or dramatic criticism, there are also principles of musical criticism. And it certainly behooves those who love and revere this art to lose no time in seeking for the unchanging psychological grounds upon which all sane and telling criticism must firmly rest.

In the light of the analysis already made, the simplest and most direct method of proceeding will be to take up in order the elements of music, rhythm, melody, and harmony, and inquire as to their relative æsthetic value, and for the criteria of worth for each in its own proper sphere.

2. So far as the analysis has gone, it goes to show that of these three elements of music, rhythm in its absolute æsthetic value ranks lowest in the scale. That it has a legitimate place and an important function in music is not to be denied, that it possesses unusual power as a stimulus for the emotional consciousness is also quite evident; but in itself considered, and for its own sake, its artistic worth is not proportionate to its emotional effectiveness. That it has an important place also in the economy of the vital processes of life has been shown to be a well-established fact, but biological standards of value are not artistic standards, nor are they interchangeable. In fact its emotional effectiveness and the striking reflex response it elicits from the listener are doubtless the source of the popular misapprehension as to its inherent artistic value. A brief résumé of the essential facts brought out in our analysis will suffice to justify the conclusion that it is distinctly below melody and harmony qualitatively considered.

Susceptibility to rhythm, it has been shown, is instinctive and the response elicited is more reflex than reflective. This, it is needless to say, is an attribute belonging to the order of lower organic reactions, not to those of the higher, more intellectual type. The basis for the one is in nerve centres controlling muscular action, while the basis for the other is in the higher centres connected, we know not how, with the functioning of mind in its more abstractly intellectual and emotional activities.

It does not require any strenuous intellectual activity to respond to the palpable rhythm of "ragtime" or the popular waltz or two-step. The mind, under the stimulus of such music, is essentially passive, stimulated to an emotional activity, but in a *meaningless* way. In such music the melody is usually but indifferently good or positively poor, though whichever it is, the strong rhythm overshadows it so that it loses its effect. And as to the harmonic factor Parry says, "Dance music demands very little in the way of harmony. The world would go on dancing to the end of time without it; and whatever harmony is added to pure dance tunes, even in days of advanced art, is generally of the simplest and most obvious character." Reaction to rhythm, therefore, though strongly emotional, is an activity containing only a minimum of genuine intellectual elements, and is in this respect distinctly below both melody and harmony.

That rhythm serves but a subordinate function in art is further established by the fact that it relates more to the *form* of a work of art than to its content, and that alone it has little or no real artistic value. Rhythm can enhance the artistic value of a poem, for example, but the rhythm without the thought is meaningless. Rhythm is essential to the dance, but without the animated living forms it loses all its charm; the rhythmic movement of machinery in itself does not fascinate or produce any lasting æsthetic emotion. In the same way rhythm in music, though it has its proper function and heightens the artistic effect produced, does so by putting its stamp upon a content that is in itself genuinely intellectual. Rhythm alone, as found in the most primitive forms of music, is not art but merely an effective mode of emotional stimulation. The truth we are interested to stress will be clearer from a possible classification of music based upon the presence and value of rhythm alone.

3. First, music of the primitive sort, preponderatingly rhythmical, either in monotone or with simple melodic figures, which, repeated over and over, serve to further accentuate the rhythmic element. Second, music in which both melodic or harmonic factors are found, and yet in which the rhythmic element is still predominant, as in popular music and in dance tunes referred to above. Third, music in which the rhythmic factor is still pronounced, and yet not so powerful as to overshadow the melodic and harmonic elements which are here of a higher order than in music belonging to the preceding classes. Under this head would come many of the world's national songs, like *Die Wacht am Rhein*, *La Marseillaise*, etc., marches and spirited music of the higher order. The essential difference between music of this class and of the class just preceding is that here there is a logical and an artistic justification for the rhythm in which the composition is written, while in the former case there is not. For example, the heroic element is an integral part of patriotism, and music representing this fine feeling should reflect this essential element; the pronounced rhythm does this, though not to the exclusion of melodic and harmonic virtues. Consequently the pronounced rhythm is not an intrusion, or a meaningless excitation, but a part of a consistent artistic idea. Then fourth, and finally, there is music in which the rhythm is less pronounced, more subtle but still serves a definite

artistic function. Here as before the rhythmic factor exists not merely as an effective means of emotional excitation, but as a most delicate, most subtle instrument for stimulating the emotions in their most refined nuances. The end of rhythm in such music is to accentuate the beauty of the structural element by a direct control of the mood under which this beauty will be most effectively apprehended. It thus serves a definite and an important artistic purpose.

Music of the first class, dependent upon rhythm almost exclusively for its effect, as a matter of fact has no just claim to be placed in the category of art at all. Its function is not artistic, but mere emotional excitation of the cruder sort.

Music of the second class, in which the rhythmic factor is still predominant, at the expense of melodic and harmonic elements, marks a step in musical development, but hardly a transition to the true realm of art. It is true that in music of this class the melody may be "catchy," and clever, as it was for example in the hilarious *Hiawatha*, a composition that lived both broadly and vigorously for a time, but only briefly. The rhythm in such music is still obtrusive and forms the principal source of its attraction and charm. But such forms of stimulation soon pall, and music that depends for its charm upon such a factor soon goes to a deserved oblivion. In any true form of art there must be elements of perduring worth, truth that wakes to perish never, beauty that time cannot destroy. Such truth, such beauty is not found, or has not been found as yet, by emphasizing the rhythmic factor at the expense of the other two elements of music.

In music of the third class there is a balancing of musical factors that leans more to the side of art. The rhythm is still plainly evident, but it is not the dominating element as heretofore. The *principality* now lies in the melodic and harmonic factors and the rhythm is used—and this is the redeeming fact— not merely to excite the mind for the sake of the excitation, as alcoholic beverages are sometimes taken, but for the sake of producing a definite result as was shown above. It now has a true artistic *raison d'être.*

In the last division of our classification this use is further exemplified, only in more subtle forms. Thus it passes from the primitive function of a crude emotional excitant and becomes a legitimate element of art, but, as has been said, its function is even here a subordinate one, and to over-emphasize it for the sake of its emotional effectiveness, is to be false to the first principles of true art.

4. Our psychological examination of melody led us to the conclusion that it is *par excellence* the thought element in music. It is true that there is in the higher forms of music an intellectual element in rhythm, and that harmony like melody is a pure product of the creative imagination. Notwithstanding this fact, however, the analogy between melody and conceptual thought is more extended and more vital than it is between these other elements of music. Melody, like conceptual thought, is indissolubly connected with time relations, both being inherently phenomena *in time.* Musical phrases and periods, essentially melodic factors, like the elements of language, follow each other successively; also, they stand in definite ascertain-

able—shall we not say—logical relations to each other, successive phrases and periods amplifying, illustrating, expounding the principal theme or subject. The bond which unites them into an æsthetic whole is also closely akin to the abstract bond that unifies the elements of discursive thought. In neither is the source of unity a datum of sense, but an abstract relationship, to be detected and appreciated only through the functioning of the higher powers of mental activity.

Historically, also, the conclusion that melody is the most distinctive thought element in music is justified. Before harmony was born the principles of melody resting upon the tonal relations of the scale were firmly established, and the principles of structural unity fully recognized. The introduction and development of harmony as an additional element in music did not invalidate or obviate the position melody had held as the thought element of music. Harmony was utilized to enrich melody, not to supplant it. Thus the primacy of melody as the thought element in music has not been lost. Whether or not an exception to this fact is found in the more radical forms of modern music is a point we shall not here engage to decide. When it shall have been more definitely shown that this movement is in the direction of permanent advance, there will be time enough to examine this question further.

In characterizing the melodic element in music as the thought element of this art, we have ascribed to it a high place in the scale of musical values. Though its thought content is not the sole, nor the ultimate test of a work of art, a work of art can hardly be a masterpiece unless it represents some truth of commanding importance. Great art is a vision of some great truth, and truth is a relation apprehended and appreciated through the cognitive powers of the mind. Art is not truth for truth's sake, and yet, as has been shown, significance is one of the most important æsthetic attributes. Art without thought significance is almost sure to be vapid, ephemeral, and soon becomes a weariness to the flesh, not a source of mental inspiration and delight. Moreover, it must not be forgotten that the appreciation of thought relations is the source of an æsthetic pleasure, pure and permanent, not to be gained by an appeal to the more dramatic elements of sense.

Applied to the case in hand, this means that music that lays stress upon the melodic factor, music whose palpable virtues are melodic, is superior in artistic worth to that which emphasizes chiefly the rhythmic element. Intrinsically, melody is of higher worth than rhythm or of any of the purely sensuous elements. This is not said to disparage the sense elements, but to exalt the thought content. This does not mean that rhythm does not have its proper and indispensable function, nor that simple melodic music is the highest type of music; it does mean, however, that music that accentuates the thought element, that finds its value whether in simple beautiful melody or in the more complex development of theme or motive, is on a higher plane than music that appeals primarily to strong instinctive tendencies in man, such as rhythm, or to other sensuous qualities of sound as sound. Music that emphasizes these sensuous, dramatic elements will almost certainly be both effective and popular, but if this is all, or the principal source of its appeal, it fails to measure up to the standard and dignity of a true work of art.

5. But this, however, is only the starting-point; for further progress suitable standards applicable to each individual composition must be agreed upon.

The nature of these criteria of value for melody is determined by the nature of melody itself. In the chapter above dealing with this subject such criteria have already been enumerated. If we accept the conclusion there maintained, that melody is in a unique way the thought element in music, then these criteria of melodic value are the criteria of the thought value of any other work of art. The value of any melody, therefore, or of any thought element in music, is to be determined by examining it with reference to its unity, its originality, its significance. its strength, its gracefulness, etc. The way in which these attributes will be expressed in music will be different from their expression in the other arts, but this does not alter their character nor their psychological effect. They can be taken, therefore, for the criteria of value in music just as they are accepted as the criteria of value in any other form of art.

The relation of these attributes to one another, the proportion in which they shall exist in works of artistic merit, cannot be definitely fixed. There is the greatest freedom and variation as to just which quality in a given work of art shall be predominant, and to what extent the others shall be present and how much they shall be emphasized. However, certain general conclusions can be formulated and affirmed with confidence. It is safe to say, for example, that no one of these qualities alone, to what-

ever marked degree it may be present, is sufficient
to give a composition standing as a masterpiece nor
even as a work of art. Unity will not suffice, nor
originality, nor grace, nor strength, nor any other
one attribute, however important it may be. Originality may be the vagaries of a disordered brain;
unity is an attribute of logical as well as of artistic
significance; profundity of thought is a quality of
value, but it may be altogether independent of art.

And so we might go through the list but never find
in any one of these attributes the secret of a true
art conception. Unity is perhaps of them all the
only one that is really indispensable. The others
may be important, and each will add something of
æsthetic value not provided for in any other way;
but gracefulness may take the place of originality
and strength, or significance in the subject matter
may so excuse blatant faults in the elements of style
that the work though marred is esteemed immortally great. Thus it is obviously true that a work
of art is not to be judged according to any fixed rule
or pattern. Every work of art, being a true work of
creation, must be judged for its own value. There
are no *patterns* in art, though we are endeavoring
to establish certain principles. Because of the rich
and varied character of these æsthetic elements
there is always the possibility for some new and
forceful combination. Thus new movements in
art, new schools rise now and then to disturb our
narrow and fixed preconceptions, surprise or shock
us for the time by their unfamiliarity, but soon
are given a place in our ideas of what true art may
include. The standard of art in its details is not
a fixed, but a developing ideal. Elements that may

be approved to-day are obsolete to-morrow, and those which meet with invective to-day are hailed as precursors of a great movement to-morrow. There is no way accurately to gauge popular approval in these details, but the principles of art fixed in the mind are inviolable, unchangeable, the bed-rock upon which criticism must firmly take its stand.

6. The comparative value of harmony in the trinity of musical elements is also to be determined by its inherent character and by what it adds to music. A cursory survey of its place in modern music leaves the impression that it is second in importance neither to rhythm nor to melody. Is it not to the harmonic element that modern music owes its distinction, and in it finds its greatest possibilities for development and for beauty ? Is it not in this element that the modern world finds its sole claim to have originated and developed a new form of art ? Take from modern music all that harmony gives, and all the glory and most of the beauty are gone forever; and this not merely because modern music has been conceived and written under the form of harmony, but because harmony adds to music elements of beauty and power that can be found nowhere else. Thus it would appear, that since modern music is the highest manifestation of the musical art, and modern music finds its essential characteristics inseparably bound up with harmony, harmony *ipso facto* is the element of superlative worth. But such a general line of argument, though it is not without its value, is not sufficient for the present discussion. We must look at the matter, therefore, from another point of view.

What, as a matter of fact, has harmony added to music, and what is the true valuation of such elements ?

In the chapter on Harmony it was asserted that harmony (1) adds sensuous beauty to music, (2) that it serves to enrich melody, and (3) that it forms, as it were, a new medium in which musical thought is conceived and expressed. If such are the uses of harmony in modern music, its artistic value must lie therein, and can be evaluated approximately by noticing the æsthetic significance of each.

Since every work of art must be a concrete, sensuous form, there must be some virtue inherent in these sensuous attributes indispensable for a truly æsthetic reaction. The Law of Gravitation and Kepler's Laws of Motion as forms of thought are beautiful conceptions in the abstract, but they are not works of art, nor do they suffice to produce a genuinely æsthetic experience; they are too abstract, too impersonal, to produce the warmth and vigor requisite for such experience. Or again, though the sublime in art can be gained only by the representation of some profound truth of life, some representation of an inner human experience, the representation itself must be made in some concrete, individual form. Great art must be an expression of a great truth, and yet it is worthy of note that the masterful, artistic representation of sensuous attributes in themselves and for their own sake is a very common and withal a legitimate justification of a very large number, if not, indeed, the majority of the pictures we find in modern exhibitions. Color, light and shadow, atmosphere, perspective, drawing, compositions, etc., are the aim and end of thousands upon thousands of paintings found in our galleries to-day.   Van Dyke's *Art for Art's Sake*, to mention a well-known treatise on art, leaves the impression that this is even the greater part of art. Nor is this aspect of the subject trivial or unimportant.   Great colorists in all the roll of painters, we are told, are but a scanty dozen or so, because of the inherent difficulty of mastering even this one sensuous attribute.   And its value when attained is, from the painter's point of view, fully commensurate with the difficulty of its attainment. Thus in painting, certainly, the sensuous side of this art is of sufficient importance to merit the highest consideration and to serve as a proper sphere of effort for the talent and energies of the artist.

And yet it is to be remembered that the great masterpieces that rise to the sublime touch a deeper strain.   But in itself the sensuous is important, though not sublime.

Thus while it is evident that we cannot give to harmony because of the increased sensuous beauty it gives to music the first place in the scale of musical value, it is proper to recognize its legitimate function and not to disparage what is beautiful merely because it is sensuous.

The second use of harmony given, viz., enrichment of melody, also fails to show that harmony has any clear title to precedence in the evaluation of the elements of music.   The phrase itself suggests that it serves only in a subordinate position, that instead of expressing the essence of music it is used more as a decorative feature.   It adds to the beauty and value of music, but it does so by enhancing the value of an element that is more elemental and, presumably, more fundamental.

There remains, however, one other claim of harmony to be examined, namely, its value as a new medium of musical thought and expression.

That the richness, the fulness, the power, the beauty, and even the thought content of an art depend vitally upon the medium in which it is expressed is a conclusion that admits of little doubt. Illustrations of this truth are legion, examples being found not only in the case of every art, but also in the wider field of all linguistic expression. The arts each have their own proper subjects because of the nature of the medium in which that art finds expression. We shall let one illustration suffice.

In painting, the principal idea, the thought content, can usually be expressed in black and white, that is, without the aid of color. Prints and photographs of the Madonnas of Raphael or of the frescoes of Michael Angelo, for example, if carefully studied, will enable one who has never seen the originals to get a fairly accurate and adequate conception of the thought and genius of these two masters. Even without the color—which most of us without training would not appreciate—the ideas and ideals of these two men are obvious enough. But even so, we do not compass the whole purpose and province of painting; all the beauty, the harmony, the vital touch which color gives is of course denied to him who thus becomes acquainted with art. If not all that they prize and strive in the concrete to realize, so much is gone that artists themselves would feel that such a method of studying art is most fragmentary and incomplete. The difficulty is that color is a new medium that defies adequate description or representation. For the new elements it introduces and for the effect they produce upon the mind there is no substitute The vitality due to color, the color-harmony, the sensuous effect of the color scheme, are all integral parts of the artist's conception, and without color all of these are irreparably lost.

The same principle applies to music, though even in a more vital way. Harmony not only adds to the sensuous beauty of music, and accentuates and augments the beauty and force of the melodic factor, but it furnishes music with a new element. a new medium, in which ideas are conceived, wrought out to more varied, more perfect forms, and expressed. As a new element it has its own inherent attributes and laws, but it also opens up new possibilities for musical thought. In it musicians have found such opportunities for development and for the elaboration of new forms of beauty that it has indeed been, in this respect, not the means of inaugurating a new departure in music, but the means of creating what is essentially a new art. It has made possible sensuous beauty never before even dreamed of, it has brought to melody the richest boon; but, more than that, it has revealed a new world of musical relationships, in which musicians find the richest beauty, the most profound thought, the most perfect works of art. It is in this revelation of a new world for musical thought that its true greatness lies, and here that it can best justify its claim to be the highest element in music So completely has harmony conquered the field, so universal has the custom become of conceiving musical thought in terms of harmony, such is the wealth of new musical relation it alone makes possible, that we must admit its exalted worth. This does not mean, however, that it is to possess the field solely and completely, or that the principles of musical form, principles essentially melodic in character, are now or ever will be obsolete. Color has not obviated form in painting, but only enabled it to realize its latent possibilities. And so it will be in music; harmony has not superseded melodic form, but only opens up the way through which music as a form of thought is to manifest its highest æsthetic worth.

7. In conclusion, we pause to look back over the way our argument has led and to gather up the threads that have now and then appeared throughout the discussion. If some of the conclusions seem trite and without significance, let it be remembered that they are given not so much for instruction as for doctrine, to show that the principles thus formulated apply to the whole field of music, and not merely to music in its more specialized forms.

We conclude: (1) *that the true goal of music is not found in its sensuous impressiveness.* It has been shown that music due to the medium of its expression and to the biological significance of that medium has remarkable dramatic power, that it thus has a direct and potent influence over consciousness not equalled in any other art. This influence, depending upon racial factors, is inherited and therefore instinctive. There is opportunity, therefore, by means of these various factors, for playing upon the emotions with the most intense and demonstrative effect. But the true goal of music does not lie in this direction; to regard this sensuous impressive-ness as the measure of musical worth is plainly to revert to primitive standards and to give up allegiance to the ideals of thought for which the race has contended and striven through long cycles of mental development. The standards of highest worth in art are not independent of the ideals in other realms of thought, but, on the contrary, dependent upon them in the most intimate way. To look for the ideals of music in its sensuous impressiveness, therefore, is to be false to the first principles of mental growth.

The true function of sensuous impressiveness in music is closely analogous to the place of pleasure in ethics. Pleasure is a good and not to be despised, except as it conflicts with some higher standards of value. It is only when it would arrogate to itself the honor of the *highest good* that it deserves the condemnation of the ascetic. As a *means* it is to be highly esteemed; it is a witness of physical welfare, a safeguard to health, a spur to action, and an incentive to right conduct. But as the end, the *Summum Bonum*, its dignity, its inherent psychological character, its transient nature, its independence of the intellect in so many forms, all declare its inadequacy. So it is with sensuous impressiveness in music. In itself it is a source of pleasure, a source of power; but let it try to assume the dignity of the true end, and at once its lower birth and character make it the object of attack for the merest novice in the principles of psychological and philosophical analysis.

(2) *Though in itself eminently desirable, and from the aesthetic point of view valuable, even sensuous*

beauty is not the end of music nor the final test of the musical worth of a composition. By sensuous beauty we comprehend such elements as the beauty and charm of simple melody, the consonance and increased sound beauty of harmony, timbre, palpable conformity to the elemental requirements of musical form, the simpler forms of balance, etc. It is upon the issue involved in this point that the musician and the philosopher are apt to differ radically. This, it will be remembered, was the question upon which the two schools, the Formalists and the Expressionists, were divided. To ascribe the real end of music to sensuous beauty is to over-emphasize the objective attributes at the expense of its psychological or subjective qualities. But this you urge is no argument; as well place the final criteria of worth in the objective as the subjective. True enough if this were the whole truth. The fact is, however, that these objective attributes do not have meaning or value, except as interpreted as symbolic for the needs of the perceiving mind. Then, again, it is true that though developed to the highest degree, without some deep significant thought content, these sensuous qualities will not suffice to place a work in the highest rank. Their effect upon the mind is too fleeting, too ephemeral, too superficial to represent the deepest truth in art.

(3) *The analysis made, all goes to show that in the evaluation of musical factors the virtues of musical form rank high.* In the first place, it is impossible to have content without form; and in order that the content may be readily and easily apprehended— an essential requirement in art—it must be expressed in an intelligible, pleasing manner. Form,

therefore, is the indispensable condition for the proper expression of thought. Again, form in music is what order, proportion, symmetry are in architecture, or what logical development is in the drama or the novel; it is the plan, the logical arrangement of parts, the structural order, the system that redeems musical compositions from being disjointed, heterogeneous, chaotic, meaningless, babels of sound, and makes them definite, intelligible, organized, unified works of art. Form, therefore, is not only a precondition for the expression of thought, but a form of thought itself and as such productive in the mind of a pure, intellectual form of æsthetic emotion.

(4) *The final test (not the sole one, however) of the value of a musical composition is the inherent worth of its thought content.*   Just as in literature no virtues of style have ever sufficed, independent of a deep, significant thought content, to give first rank to literary productions, so in music the ultimate test of greatness is the worth of the thought expressed. Of such manifest importance to consciousness are the things pertaining to itself that it ascribes highest value only to those qualities and attributes which plainly relate to its own aims and ends.   Call it anthropomorphism or egoism or an inherent prejudice of consciousness, or whatever you will, the fact remains that qualities and attributes are thus evaluated.   The whole trend of art and of art development to a certain extent justifies this procedure, for from its inception until now art has to a larger and larger degree found its proper content, not in mere objective forms, but in subjective ideas and ideals.   Literature develops from the epic to the drama, from mere descriptions of objective

scene or act to the most subtle psychological analysis of motives, of consciousness, and of character. Painting passes from the crude representation of form and action to the representation of the deepest emotions and the most profound depths of character. Music also has followed the same line of progress and has led from an undue stress given to sense elements, to a form of art in which genuine thought relations are the mark of the highest worth.

What some of these thought relations are has been pointed out in our discussion of the æsthetic attributes of music. To form correct judgments of musical value, to apply the standards we have attempted to enumerate, is the proper work of the musical critic, not of the student of musical æsthetics. We leave this aspect of the problem, therefore, to those to whom it properly belongs.

There is one caution, however, to which attention must be called before we conclude. While we have thus introduced distinctions of worth among the various attributes and qualities of music, this does not imply that any one is sufficient in itself, or that others lower down in the scale do not exert a proper and an important æsthetic function. On the other hand, it were truer to fact to say that just so far as a work of art fails to exemplify *all* of these attributes, just so far does it fail to attain to the perfect fulness and beauty and significance and power of the ideal of art.

CHAPTER XI

1. In these days of the practical even in the very heart of philosophical discussion, there is little need to excuse the introduction of a concluding chapter upon the practical or educational value of music. It will certainly do no harm to the sanctity of the theoretical if it can be made to serve as the basis for some suggestions by means of which its truth will bear fruit in actual life. Indeed, the theoretical and the practical should be so correlated that each will supplement and complete the other. They are both essential parts of the complete envisagement of a subject. Theory without practice is but futile speculation; practice without theory puerile experimentation. Practice needs to be guided by theory to attain the best results, and theory should be checked by experience, if it is not to lose itself in empty generalities. Hence it is eminently fitting before we bring our discussion to a close, that we desert for a time the goal that has guided us thus far, and frankly turn our faces toward the practical. This we shall do by endeavoring to estimate the educational value of music.

Attention has already been called to the large place which music now holds in our social, educational, artistic, and religious life, and reasons given to explain its importance. Starting with this same fact, we shall now inquire, *cui bono ?* To what end ? What does music bring to the individual or to society to justify the enormous expenditure of time and energy now devoted to its cultivation ? Not only are millions of dollars expended annually in our larger cities for its artistic development—that in itself were a matter of little importance—but on every hand we see the "precious plastic period of youth" in our schools and out of them being expended that it may have even a greater part in our social and intellectual life. Can it justify its place in our already overcrowded courses of study, and in taking the time that might be devoted to more practical pursuits ?

The answer to these questions can be found only in a careful inquiry as to the true educational value of music. But before we are ready to discuss the subject intelligently, we must have before us some definite conception of the proper function of education. For as an object has value only in relation to some *end* to be attained, so a subject in a course of study must be appraised in relation to the ideal of education itself. Before we can say, therefore, whether music has educational value, the purpose of educational discipline must be stated. In so doing we must necessarily be somewhat dogmatic, for there is here no opportunity to support our definition by argument. To meet the present need, we premise that education is that mental discipline and growth by which a man is prepared to enter intelligently and sympathetically into the most important forms of human thought and action, and to attain for himself maximum efficiency in some useful line of human endeavor. It is in the light of some such comprehensive conception of education as this that the educational value of music must be considered and its value determined.

2. In seeking to get a clear idea of the practical value of music as a method of educational discipline it is natural, and it will be helpful to turn first to that people whose educational maxim for centuries was, "Gymnastics for the body, music for the mind." And not only was this the maxim of Athens in the days of her glory, but it was through following this method of education that she attained to her exalted place as the world's preceptress in so many branches of learning and of art. It is true that with the Greeks the term music included more than it does with us to-day, but it is also true that no small part of the training of their youth consisted in learning to improvise upon the lyre a rhythmical and melodious accompaniment to passages of Homer. The teacher of music—music in this technical sense—had his place with the teacher of reading. So even in the restricted sense of the term, their "music" was largely musical; that is, a training in rhythm and in melody. We to-day have no training comparable to their training in these two subjects

As to the value which they attributed to this kind of training there can be no question. Listen to the words of Plato, who but expressed the current belief of his time: "We would not have our guardians grow up amid images of moral deformity, as in some noxious-pasture, and there browse and feed upon many a baneful herb and flower day by day, little by little, until they silently gather a festering mass of corruption in their soul. Let our artists rather

be those who are gifted to discern the true nature
of the beautiful and the graceful; then will our
youth dwell in a land of health, amid fair sights
and sounds, and receive the good in everything;
beauty, the effluence of fair works, shall flow into
the eye and ear like a health-giving breeze from a
purer region, and insensibly draw the soul from
earliest youth into likeness and sympathy with the
beauty of reason." As to the best means to secure
this inward disposition of soul, he says: "Musical
training is a more potent instrument than any other,
because rhythm and harmony find their way into
the inward places of the soul, on which they mightily
fasten imparting grace and making the soul of him
who is rightly educated graceful, or of him who is
ill-educated ungraceful. And also because he who
has received this true education of the inner being
will most shrewdly perceive omissions or faults in
art and nature and with a true taste, while he praises
and rejoices ever to receive into his soul the good,
and becomes noble and good, he will justly blame
and hate the bad now in the days of his youth,
even before he is able to know the reason why;
and when reason comes, he will recognize and salute
the friend with whom his education has made him
familiar." [1]

Such was Greek education, not merely in theory,
but in actual and long-continued practice. In
what it resulted, history informs us; we still to-day
look back with wonder and admiration to see what
this people accomplished, not only in Art, in the Epic,
the Drama, in Sculpture, in Architecture, but in
other fields where mental acumen and trained powers

[1] *Republic*, III.

of discrimination are essential. Whatever the causes
may be, the fact remains that during the Periclean
age and immediately following, there was in Athens
such a coterie of poets, sculptors, dramatists, orators,
philosophers, and statesmen, as the whole world
has not equalled at any one time since. And whether
or not the musical training which the Greek youth
as a rule received be the whole explanation, it is
true that just such a training in the power of discrimination is an essential factor in producing that
sensitiveness to fine shades of difference which is
demanded not only in art, but in all the higher forms
of mental activity. On the whole, therefore, I am
inclined to believe that their musical education goes
far to explain the remarkable intellectual genius
of this people.

Aristotle, also, with his more analytic mind,
similarly approves the importance given to musical
education.[1] He goes further than Plato, and suggests definite reasons why music should be retained
as a factor in their educational procedure. In
brief, his argument can be summarized under three
heads: (1) Music should be cultivated as a desirable
form of pleasurable recreation; (2) as conducive
to mental development, and (3) for its effect upon
moral character. But we cannot accept unquestion-
ingly as advantageous for society to-day educational
practices which then may have been never so
beneficial. New social conditions, new industrial,
new ethical, new religious environment demand on
the part of the individual new adjustments, new
reactions. So while this musical training seems to
have been eminently adapted to the æsthetic and

[1] *Vid. Politics*, Book VIII.

intellectual life of the Greeks, from that fact alone there is but little assurance that, followed now, it would result in like effects. We can properly do no more than consider these facts as suggestions worthy of consideration in the light of the changed conditions of our modern environment. We shall take these suggestions of Aristotle, therefore, and see how far they can be adapted with helpfulness to modern life.

3. There is no need, I fancy, to advance argument to show that in order to obtain from the human organism, either physically or mentally, the highest results, both quantitatively and qualitatively, some form of recreation is imperative. The demand is one which has the sanction of law, both divine and scientific, and is a fact of experimental knowledge with all who have done intense or long-continued labor, whether physical or mental. In modern life, this demand has become peculiarly urgent; our social and industrial organizations have so modified the activities of life that this need is greater than ever before. In the days of simpler organization, the duties of life were different enough to satisfy the demands for variation in the form of activity for the day or the week. But to-day excessive specialization has altered this condition of labor. The highly organized condition of all departments of human activity, educational, political, industrial, has divided society into two general divisions. On the one hand, there are the few at the head of great corporations and organizations where the nerve strain of management and control is intensified by the magnitude of the interests represented; on the other hand, there is the great

mass of people condemned in their work to a life of mental inanition because of the monotony and routine required in their subordinate positions. There are the few, of course, who will rise to more responsible positions, or have other interests to keep the mind from stagnation. But the great masses cannot or will not; they will settle down in their narrow sphere and become little more than a part of the great machinery of life. And the tragedy of it is, that the closer they approach to this automatism, the better they are fitted to fulfil their part.   Such is the actual condition of thousands upon thousands employed in our factories to-day. This is a part of the price we must pay for progress. With the few, great responsibility and nerve strain, and with the many, lack of initiative and the inspiration from control, and too often a monotony in their work that blunts the sensibilities and the emotions and atrophies the intellectual faculties.

In both cases recreation is demanded to prevent disaster.   In the one case, to take the mind completely away from its cares and usual circle of activity, in the other, to stir the mind to life by something different from the ceaseless hum of machinery and from the deadening fatigue and monotony of the same action, repeated week after week, year after year. It is to break the monotony of such lives, to give opportunity for fancy, stifled in the grime of the shop, to play, and for the emotions, weighted down with the cares of a sordid reality, to rise, that we see our theaters filled by melodrama or vaudeville and stand astounded at the sale of indifferent fiction. It is not a question whether or not the people will have recreation—that is a psychological demand or protest that cannot be smothered—but what shall be the nature of their amusement. The conditions of life to-day, as they did not in a simpler society, justify the demand for radical recreation.

For this great, almost overpowering demand of the masses for some form of relaxation and relief from the tedium of their toil, music may become a veritable godsend. Notice, if you will, how well it meets the prime conditions of a good form of recreation. First, a good recreation must call into activity those mental faculties which, in the course of one's vocation, are usually dormant. Second, if it be more than a passing fad, it must be inherently pleasurable. There is an undoubted, an ascertainable physiological effect in pleasure, a stimulus to healthful metabolism, which is often more efficacious than the services of the best physician. Then, third, it must hold the mind so firmly that there is no slipping back into the old grooves of thought. It must have such inherent interest and power that the mind is, as it were, compelled to follow in these new lines of activity, leaving the fatigued centres of the brain time to recuperate and recover their vitality and power.

Music, it is needless to say, is eminently adapted in all these respects to serve as an ideal form of recreation, and to help counterbalance the emotional lifelessness which present industrial conditions make inevitable in so large a part of labor. Music, as has been so often asserted, is a direct and a powerful stimulus for the emotions and so, better than any other art, can relieve the fatigue of the day and arouse the mind from its listlessness and lassitude to pleasurable and intense emotional reaction. In such uses as this there is no need to discard the sensuous qualities which give it power. Thus it meets the first condition of a good form of recreation in the fullest manner. Music is also inherently pleasurable and so produces that beneficial effect which results from the heightened feeling tone, and also creates a taste for itself so that it may the more readily become effective as a method of relaxation and recreation.

It also claims the attention completely, so that it in fact produces that mental condition requisite for a literal re-creation of nervous force and energy. In all these respects, therefore, it meets the demands of a good form of recreation. If for no other reasons, it has to-day sufficient value, upon this ground alone, to justify its place as an important element in life, and worthy of careful and widespread cultivation.

But however strong may be the claims of music as a desirable form of recreation, education, it will be insisted, should be for the business of life rather than for the enjoyment of its leisure. Prepare for the business and the people will look out for amusement. Though this principle is plainly contrary to all psychological law and to educational theory, as well as to common sense, we are by no means limited to this one means of justifying the place of music in our educational practices. Music has value, also, as we shall now attempt to show, as a means of intellectual discipline as well as a valuable means of recreation.

4. There is a popular impression that the value of music as a means of intellectual discipline is so small that it can safely be neglected; nay, more, it

is held that the cultivation of this art is positively injurious to intellectual interests, that it leads to such excessive emotionalism, that .the stability of the judgment and of reason is seriously impaired.

The source of this misconception is now evident. It lies in the failure to discriminate properly between the two aspects of music which we have called the "dramatic" and the "æsthetic." There is such force, such dramatic impressiveness in the sensuous attributes of music, that for the untutored, untrained mind, they overshadow the less evident æsthetic qualities. Consequently, there is a tendency on the part of those not versed in the intricacies of musical structure to overlook this aspect of the subject and to regard the dramatic attributes as the characteristic elements of music. The instinctive, *quasi*-reflex response to the sensuous attributes of musical sound is mistaken for genuine musical appreciation, when in some respects they are no more alike than the tingle of pain from a burn and a scientific discussion of the molecular theory of heat. In the one case the reaction is organic, physiological, reflex, while in the other it is strictly psychical, analytic, and discriminatingly intellectual.

Were these sensuous attributes all that there is to music, there would be some justification for the popular belief just referred to; there is little educational value in simple reaction to instinctive forms of stimuli. They are by nature fitted to accomplish their purpose without the mediation of consciousness; this is what their instinctive nature signifies. But there is to music, as our analysis has plainly shown, another aspect, the possibilities of which are not to be compassed by any such simple, inattentive way. As a true form of art, music rises above the plane of primitive emotions and simple reaction to sense stimuli, to the realm of the intellectual, and of the emotions in their very purest forms. To get the thought element in music of this latter type, to appreciate the beauty of form and of formal relations, to apprehend the unity of a composition, the unity of logical structure in the midst of sensuous complexity, or to feel the proper interpretation for the subtleties of harmony, all of this opens up a new field for intellectual and emotional activity of a very complex and intricate kind. There is no dearth of opportunity here for intellectual acumen, for logical analysis, and for all the activities of æsthetic synthesis. Plainly, it is in this direction that opportunities for real and useful intellectual activity may be found.

In considering more specifically the value of music as a form of intellectual discipline, attention is called first to its possible utility as a means of ear-training. In connection with the activity of each sense there is necessarily a certain amount of mental functioning involved, discrimination incipient or explicit, comparison and judgment, etc. To develop these processes so that accuracy of observation becomes a matter of habit, is no little task nor an inconsequential form of mental attainment. The sense of hearing, next to the sense of sight, offers the greatest opportunities for development of this sort, and is second in importance only to the visual sense. Whatever mental discipline there is to be gained in the perceptual process, through the training of the sense to greater accuracy and greater sensitiveness, can be gained as readily by developing the sense of hearing as the sense of sight. And is it not possible, aside from the practical value of such training, that a greater refinement of this sense might reveal beauties around us to which most of us are habitually insensible ? While nature is doubtless richer in her visual attributes than in her auditory, there may still be something of value even for the ear if it only be trained to hear it. Why might there not be a poet of nature's voices as well as painters of her visual phases?

But of greater practical value would be the sensitiveness to tonal inflection in spoken language which such an ear-training would promote. As a matter of fact, only a few are responsive to inflection when it is heard, and only now and then do we find one who to any degree utilizes the possibilities of his voice in this direction. An increased susceptibility to the sound qualities of language would not only increase the pleasurable effect, but it would serve to promote the efficiency of spoken language for all the purposes for which it exists.

The chief source of the intellectual value of musical training, however, is to be found in connection with the more complex æsthetic attributes which belong to music by virtue of the fact that it is a true form of thought. To apprehend the unity of a musical composition of any structural complexity, such as is found in almost all good music, is an intellectual process of no trivial or insignificant character. It is the perception of a mental ideal in sensuous form, the interpretation of sense symbolism in terms of the most abstract form of thought. To pass judgment upon a composition as to its originality or its strength demands the highest degree of exact discrimination, of comparison, and of mental synthesis. The appreciation of gracefulness betokens a sensitiveness to fine distinction of form and meaning which may prove most beneficial, not only in art, but in mental processes both intellectual and moral. Whether or not intellectual discipline is to be found in the study of music, therefore, depends altogether upon the manner and purpose of such study. It may be merely a reflex response to instinctive elements, or it may be a critical analytic study which will give both acumen and balance to the intellect, and that sensitiveness to fine shades of beauty in which we as a nation with vigorous constitutions and industrial ideals are so noticeably lacking.

5. The third suggestion of Aristotle as to the educational value of music, viz., that music has a profound influence upon character, is worthy of careful notice in this connection. Is it true, as the Greeks believed, that music does in some subtle way so influence the soul that it has value as a means of developing character ? Under the Greek conception, where the *good* and the *beautiful* were so conjoined that they were almost identical, this teaching is not hard to appreciate; but in terms of our stricter discrimination between the moral and the æsthetic, can music still be utilized for moral training and moral development ?

Upon such an open question as this it is not strange that opinions directly contradictory to one another should be held and often expressed. At the one extreme there is the belief, justified by many unfortunate examples, that as a profession music is a severe strain upon character and even inherently and positively destructive of moral rectitude. On the other hand, it has been believed from the time of Aristotle until now that music and morality are not inconsistent, but are mutually helpful. Philosophers have not been slow to call attention to the fact that elements of beauty are to be found in the moral ideal, and elements of morality in the beautiful. In such extreme positions, however, there is such a noticeable lack of scientific accuracy that they serve to do little more than to call our attention to the fact that there is here a problem worthy of the most careful examination. In the first case, it is plainly nothing more than an opinion founded upon individual examples more than upon analysis; in the second, the truth is so abstract that it needs men philosophically disposed to appreciate it. The problem is too comprehensive for an adequate discussion here, though some suggestion following from our analysis of music may prove helpful.

In what has been said concerning music as a form of recreation, we have already called attention to one way in which music may be utilized for the moral uplift of society. Reforms never come by merely execrating what is disapproved, but by offering a substitute for the evil to be overcome. Especially is this true in regard to amusements and forms of recreation. All the maledictions of the just are not so potent to remove evil and keep it removed as the less exciting, more arduous labor of showing people plainly the value of things that are wholesome. Music has those attributes which adapt it to supplant many of the lower forms of amusement, and to give a taste for those things which are refined and noble and beautiful. To do this would require intelligent instruction and guidance, but there is no form of wholesome recreation that could so easily be introduced or could more readily serve as a means of bringing to the great mass of the people the pleasures and the benefits of true art ideas. If art is a work of culture, it is worth while to cultivate it among those who now know so little of its true meaning or benefits. If art in general, or music in particular, is a suitable subject to engage the thought and energies of the higher stratum of society, it is a suitable subject for cultivation by those whose intellectual attainments are not their chief source of self-congratulation.

In considering the moral aspect of music, some attention must be given to the close relation music holds to religious experience. So closely are music and religion associated that it is hard to believe that there is not some potent bond between music and the moral life. Without music religion would lose one-half its power, not because religion is less strong, but because music has the peculiar power of leading the mind to an attitude of prayer and solemn praise. The church bell may call the people to the outer courts of the temple, but it is the organ and song that purify the heart so that they may pass into the inner court where those who worship, worship in sincerity and in truth. So close is the relation in modern thought between religion and morality that in the light of these facts it is hard to believe that music does not have also some profound though subtle influence over character.

The principle according to which the question of the moral significance of music must be determined has appeared in our discussion. There is in music besides the intellectual element, which has only a nominal relation to morality, a strong emotional factor which may well be the very source and inspiration of much that is inherently and characteristically moral. We neglect, therefore, the intellectual aspects of music, though it is not altogether negligible, that we may emphasize the more the point which is most vital. We shall accept, then, as our working principle the fact, that *the moral value of music is found in the direct and powerful effect which it exerts upon the emotional consciousness.* If experience and reflection have shown that knowledge is not virtue, or even a guarantee of moral earnestness, psychological and sociological investigations have emphasized the fact that in the emotions are the springs of both moral and immoral action. It is in this line of investigation, therefore, that the solution of the riddle must be found.

More than any other art, better than almost any other mental stimulus, music, through the direct and powerful factor of rhythm, and through the inherited biological significance of sound, stimulates the mind emotionally. In this fact lie both its strength and its weakness; strength, because it can play with a master hand over the whole gamut of man's emotional life; weakness, because there is about the emotions music awakens an indefiniteness that leaves them unattached, as it were, to any conceptual thought or ideal of conduct. And as Professor James has told us, pure emotionalism tends to weaken character rather than to strengthen it. It is just here that we find the difference in the moral value of music and of the sermon in the services of the church. Music stimulates the emotions and brings the attitude of worship, but it leaves the emotions unattached to ideals of action or of conduct. The minister finds the heart, through the services of music, receptive and aglow, but he must take these emotions and connect them consciously with right actions, right thoughts, or they will evanesce and the mind that felt them intensely, it may be, will have received no permanent good. Music can awaken the emotions, but it cannot direct them or connect them with proper ideals of ethical action.

Judged in the light of the relation between the emotions and conduct, a just evaluation of the moral value is not so difficult as it might otherwise appear. Granted that the moral significance of music comes through its emotional power, it remains only to show the relation between the emotion music produces and conduct. And this fortunately is not such a very obscure psychological problem. We note first certain fundamental differences between ethical and æsthetical emotions.

The distinguishing marks of the ethical feelings are found in their *personal* character and in the authority they claim in all matters of conduct. Their right to primacy is a part of their reality; they do not advise, they do not dissuade, they regard not desires or pleasure, but they summarily and categorically dictate what ought to be done, what must be done. Interpreted for our present purposes, this means that the motor element is a dominant one. It is a part of their true character to actualize themselves in conduct. The ethical emotion of justice includes the command, "be thou just;" the feeling of mercy enjoins us to be merciful.

In all the ethical emotions there is always the feeling of personal obligation to let the sentiment bear fruit in deed.

The æsthetic emotions, on the other hand, are as truly characterized by the lack as the ethical emotions by the presence of this same personal and obligatory element. One of the first characteristics of the æsthetic experience is that we tend to project ourselves into the work of art, to lose the feeling of personal identity, as it were, by living intently for the time the conception represented. Personal self-consciousness dwindles and the artist's idea looms large in consciousness. That is, for the time we live vicariously in the conception of the artist. In the same way the feeling of obligation, the quintessence of the moral feeling, is hardly present at all in the æsthetic emotions. There are certain principles of art which are the criteria of right judgment and good taste, but they are not binding in the same uncompromising way as are ethical laws. It is more a *lack* than a positive fault if my judgments do not accord with them. The obligation I am under to regard these principles of good taste is nothing more than a conventional ought, and lacks altogether the categorical imperativeness which Kant tells us is the essence of the moral law.

Such being the case, it is evident that music, or any other form of æsthetic culture, in itself will not suffice as a system of ethical training; the emotions engendered by such experience, though varied and strong, are lacking in just that personal reference which is the vital element in all ethical experience. In order to develop moral force and stamina, the volitional nature must receive a more direct, a more heroic discipline than comes from the chance suggestion of the æsthetic sentiments. While the musician must live in the realm of the emotions largely, these emotions, being æsthetic rather than ethical in character, have only a nominal value for real moral discipline. Thus it is that we sometimes find men whose education has been largely artistic, whether musical or some other form there is little difference, who through *neglect* of these other factors are from the moral point of view ill-balanced and unstable. But the source of the trouble is not with the education they have received, but with the part that has been neglected.

We conclude, therefore, that music as a profession is not inconsistent with a thoroughly moral character, but that it alone is not sufficient for the proper training of the will implied in character. The æsthetic emotions, though strong and inspiring, lack that personal factor in the ethical sentiments which leads to their application in conduct. The difficulty, therefore, is not that art and morality are contradictory or in any way inconsistent, but merely that in the emotional life these two aspects fail to meet at the most crucial point.

Thus far we have spoken only of the limitations of music considered as a form of moral training; there is, however, a more positive aspect of the problem too important to be overlooked. Sometimes it is true, and never more frequently than in moral training, that what cannot be gained by a rigorous, logical method can be accomplished by indirect methods and without showing the iron hand that leads the way.

It is well to remember, therefore, that something

more than a rigorous training of the will, however essential that may be, is required to raise virtue from the austere sphere of law and duty to the plane of a great enthusiasm, capable of enlisting the sympathies and whole-hearted allegiance of the developed man. What is required for the most effective morality is not a constant, half-morbid self-analysis of motives, but that the individual shall lose himself, as it were, by becoming identified, heart and soul, with some great purpose in life. And high purposes, lofty ambitions, effective zeal, are born of great hopes, great emotions. The day of puritanic ideals, of constant self-denial, is past; the day when conduct is to be determined more by loyalty to some world-wide, altruistic purpose has already dawned. Thus, the part of the emotions in determining conduct is destined to be greater than ever before. And music, through its great emotional power, is peculiarly adapted to enlarge the scope of man's mind, to reveal to man the unfathomed depth of his own spirit, to awaken longings for the infinitely perfect, to create in the heart that divine harmony of mental equipoise which may give birth to inspired ambitions and to purposes of the most gloriously unselfish character.

The ethical and the æsthetical ideals, notwithstanding their points of difference, are by no means unrelated. In a very comprehensive, very forceful way it can be readily shown that the charm and attractiveness of the moral ideal is to no small extent due to its æsthetic qualities. The Good is beautiful in many profound respects. The cultivation of the æsthetic sentiments, and sensitiveness for the elements of beauty, will, as

Plato said, serve to cultivate a taste for what is wholesome and fair. Not only will music rightly used enlarge the emotional nature, making possible great enthusiasm and great ambition, but it will also prove a safeguard from what is ignoble and base. He who has a refined taste for the deeper beauty of literature or painting or music, is certainly not worse, but better prepared to be attracted by what is morally high and unselfish and motived by right principles.

If it is recalled, it will be found to be the rule that even the faults of our artistic fraternity are not the worst in the category of crime or sin. The strong emotionalism of such characters may lead to certain excesses, to such an overstepping of the conventions and customs of society that punishment must be meted out; but maliciousness and satanic heartlessness and hardness are not the ruling faults of men of this profession. So exclusively scientific and intellectual have our educational ideals and practices become, that we stand much in need of some subjects which will develop in its finer reactions the emotional side of human nature. Music properly used is eminently adapted to fill such a place in our educational practice.

6. But the question now arises, are we in our current use of music utilizing it to the best advantage? Music, in our system of schools, is being taught, on the whole, efficiently; is not this training adapted, and adequate to meet all the requirements of the best educational interests?

There are two principal reasons why this training as now given in our schools is not entirely adequate to meet the demand we have the right to expect from the place it holds in our educational practice.

In the first place, the training there given is for the most part, if not entirely, vocal; and while this is important, it will not serve to open up to the pupils the best treasures of modern music. I doubt whether the training in reading music, such as is given in our schools, will go very far toward making the pupils appreciative listeners to music of the better class. It is all essential, but not adequate.

Then, again, and this is by far the weightier reason, there is such a profound difference between a capacity to sing or to play correctly, and a refined and appreciative musical taste, that something should be done to insure the latter as well as to cultivate the former. We are not so inconsistent, fortunately, in regard to literature. We do not believe that the ability to read intelligently will give a taste for Shakespeare, or Browning, or Tennyson, when the more exciting forms of story and novel are at the hand of the pupil. We have learned that the only way to cultivate a taste for good literature is to study the masterpieces and to become acquainted with their richness of thought and beauties of expression. Taste for an author is developed only by studying his works, and for good literature only by becoming acquainted with it. The teaching of music in our schools must necessarily be of the rudiments and without sufficient time to lead up through technical knowledge to a correct taste for the highest and best in music. This may be possible in musical schools and conservatories, but manifestly not in the public schools. Consequently, the question arises whether something more directly in the line of cultivating a good taste might not be undertaken with profit? The importance of good taste here is hard to over-emphasize. As compared with technical skill or knowledge, it should be much the more strongly insisted upon. Skill may be employed on what is idle and useless as well as upon what is beautiful and helpful. But once good taste is acquired, we have introduced an ever-potent, uplifting influence, which will not only point to the upward road, but will lead toward what is refined and noble, and so elevating both morally and intellectually. Taste in the æsthetic world is what character is in the moral world, a settled principle of choice, a habitual and proper method of responding to stimuli. What is needed, therefore, if we are to derive the best returns from musical education, is that there be some general attempt to raise the standard of musical taste so that there will be a wider appreciation of music of this higher sort.

An objection likely to be raised by musicians to any such plan as this is that there is no other way to musical appreciation than the road through technical musical knowledge. While we grant the value of such knowledge, and are only restrained from urging this as the proper gateway to musical appreciation by the many demands made upon our time and energy by an ever-increasing course of study, we still contend that there is a shorter road that will greatly increase our appreciative knowledge of music, though it may be entirely inadequate for a critical knowledge. Not every one who enjoys Shakespeare on the stage is fitted to be a dramatic critic, nor is the average reader of poetry, he who reads it for the pure pleasure it brings, always capable of stating explicitly just the source of the pleasure he finds. On the whole, it is an open question just how far an exact, critical knowledge of an art stands in direct proportion to the pleasure it gives. And the advantages we are interested to secure are those which come partly through enjoyment—an appreciative enjoyment—not through a critical knowledge of art.

Let us, then, accept as the practical method of securing these benefits the method used in securing like results in literature, the only other art seriously studied in the schools. The way to cultivate a taste for good music is to hear it, to have it explained so as to be able to recognize the various elements introduced, their nature and their use. Can this be done, you ask, except through a musical education ? We believe that it can, and shall conclude our discussion by offering a suggestion for a simple, easy, economical method of securing these eminently desirable results.

Let the pupils of our secondary schools and the students in our higher institutions of learning have an hour once a week, or even once in two weeks, devoted to music in this practical way, and I am sure the results would more than justify the expense in time and money. Let them *hear* good music and have its structural and æsthetic attributes pointed out to them, as attention is called to the elements of beauty in a work of literature, and they will learn to appreciate good music as they learn to appreciate good literature. Let them hear it in properly graded series, not once or twice, but often enough to get acquainted with it to recognize the more obvious characteristics, and a taste for what is artistic and what is valuable can be formed. A few hundred dollars a year would provide a teacher in this new work, for only the hour would be required, and the other work of the school would not lose but gain from a period devoted to the cultivation of a taste for what is in the best sense beautiful. Thus might the benefits now confined to the chosen few be made the common possession of thousands, to whom the true beauty of music is now a riddle they cannot solve, a mystery they cannot understand.

BIBLIOLIFE

Old Books Deserve a New Life
www.bibliolife.com

Did you know that you can get most of our titles in our trademark **EasyScript**™ print format? **EasyScript**™ provides readers with a larger than average typeface, for a reading experience that's easier on the eyes.

Did you know that we have an ever-growing collection of books in many languages?

Order online:
www.bibliolife.com/store

Or to exclusively browse our **EasyScript**™ collection:
www.bibliogrande.com

At BiblioLife, we aim to make knowledge more accessible by making thousands of titles available to you – quickly and affordably.

Contact us:
BiblioLife
PO Box 21206
Charleston, SC 29413

Lightning Source UK Ltd.
Milton Keynes UK
UKOW031318170413

209368UK00003B/72/P

9 781110 618880